THE ULTIMATE GAME COOKBOOK

Tom Bridge

PIATKUS

Dedication
For Doreen Fitzpatrick.
A very special lady.

© 1999 by Tom Bridge

Designed by Sara Kidd
Illustrations by Madeleine David

First published in 1999 by
Judy Piatkus (Publishers) Limited
5 Windmill Street
London W1P 1HF

This paperback edition published in 2000

The moral right of the author has been asserted

A *catalogue record of this book is available
from the British Library*

ISBN 0 7499 2093 9

Printed and bound in Great Britain by Butler & Tanner Ltd, Frome and London

Cover photographs: left and middle picture courtesy of Photodisc Photolibrary
Right-hand picture courtesy of Fayre Game

Acknowledgements

This book has been one of the most interesting projects I have undertaken. Very special thanks are due to Michael Virtue and Russums, who talked me into this two-year project. Michael mentioned to me that there are very few good game cookery books on the market, and asked why I didn't write one; hence this mouthwatering collection. Thanks also to my dear friend Louisa Ayland from the Game Marketing Executive, Executive Chairman Peter Pearce and Marketing Director Kevin O'Sullivan of Fairfax Meadow who have now taken game products on board – and with a customer-base that reads like a *Who's Who* of the catering and food industry, they are surely on to a winning idea. I do hope my *Ultimate Game Cookbook* goes a long way in helping to provide new ideas for the Food Service Industry.

Thanks are also due to Klinge Foods, the makers of Lo-Salt, which is the only salt I use throughout this book; Brian Hargreaves, my favourite wine taster and food writer for *Life* magazine; Graham Portwine and Joseph from Pegs Club in Covent Garden, London; Nick White at Ashwood Fine Foods who provided me with a great deal of the game meat required to write this book; wonderful Alice Portnoy and Caroline at Neff Marketing for all their help and for supplying the Neff kitchen equipment which I now duly depend on to create these delicious recipes at my cottage; Bob Kennard at Graig Farm; Christina Baskervile and Nigel Dauncey of Barrow Boar in Yeovil; my dear friends Peter Young and Peter Kay from Openshaws in Bolton (and his very tiny son Ollie) who is Rediveg; The Cairns family; Ark Foods in Diss; Fayre Game in St Helens; Mike Robbins at the Hart of England Deer Farm in Warwick; Brian Olverson who is Red Velvet; David and Laura Lam who are Mrs Lam's Delicious Food Company in Liverpool and all the staff at Makentie.

To write this book I had to do some travelling, and a big thank you firstly to Tony Tymon at British Airways in Manchester, and to the finest staff at the finest hotels in England: Dee Ludlow from the Duchess of Duke Street; The Cavendish at St James's, London; The Waldorf; Julian Groom at Le Meridian in Poona, India (good luck for your new venture – a long way to travel for a curry but worth it!); Malcolm and Julie McHardy at Nunsmere Hall Country House Hotel, Cheshire; Carol and Michael Fletcher at The Nanny Brow Country House Hotel; Lauder Grange Hotel in Corbridge, Northumberland, and to all my fellow chefs who are too numerous to mention.

Thanks also to everyone at Transmedia UK, especially Kerry and Nick who keep me on my toes; Granada Television's Kimberley Hughes and Run Rabbit Run, Carlton Food Network and Ali Hilmini at Harrods.

Final thanks go to David Hinds who collects all of my cookery books; Mr and Mrs Simon Machin at British Telecom, but most of all to my wife Jayne and my boys Gareth and Matthew.

Lastly, thanks to everyone at Piatkus for having faith in my work.

CONTENTS

Acknowledgements 3

Introduction 6

1. BIRDS OF A FEATHER 9

Duck 12 Grouse 47

Pheasant 24 Guinea fowl 51

Partridge 30 Goose 56

Quail 36 Wild turkey 59

Pigeon 43

2. FIRST CATCH YOUR HARE 65

Rabbit 66

Hare 74

3. THE THRILL OF THE CHASE 79

Venison 80

Wild boar 91

4. SOMETHING FISHY 99

Salmon 100

Trout 106

5. SOUPS 109

6. PIES, TERRINES AND PATES 117

7. BASICS AND ACCOMPANIMENTS 139

Appendix 155

Recommended game suppliers and useful information 155

Index 158

INTRODUCTION

In writing this book I have had various aims in view: to familiarize the reader with the different types of game available on the British market; to explain game preparation and cookery for those who have not tried it before; and to present the reader with a wide number of delicious recipes – my own favourite international dishes, given to me by fellow chefs and interspersed with recipes I have devised and developed for myself and for various companies throughout the UK and Europe. Most of these recipes use game that is readily available.

The term 'game' was traditionally used only for those wild birds and animals that were hunted and eaten, such as pigeon, partridge, pheasant, rabbit and venison. Farmed game is now widely available from butchers and supermarkets, and includes venison, guinea fowl and quail. Wild game is subject to legal shooting seasons (see the table on page 7), but farmed game can be available all year round. You can buy wild game from specialist suppliers, wholesale markets, or direct from a shoot or estate which has a selling licence. For a list of suppliers, including mail order, see page 155.

If you buy game from a supermarket, oven-ready, it will probably be mild in flavour. The strong flavour that most people associate with game comes from 'hanging', which is generally done to increase tenderness. How mild or strong you like your game is something you will find out by trying it. User-friendly cuts of game are being sold more widely: pheasant suprêmes, for example, or diced rabbit for casseroles, or boned quails. And it is perfect for the barbecue.

Game has been eaten for centuries all over Europe, but has become much more popular over the last few years. It is easy to cook, full of flavour, and adaptable to all kinds of recipes. Wild game is also very low in fat – pheasant, for example, has around 2.5 per cent fat, rabbit around 3 per cent. This is of great interest to those who are concerned to follow a healthy diet. It is high in protein and low in cholesterol.

In this book you will find a wide variety of recipes, from the traditional ones like roast duck and venison to more modern ones such as stir-fries, curries and salads. The combination of quick cooking with low-fat healthy meat and fish is one which is sure to appeal.

The final chapter in the book deals with some of the traditional methods of cooking game –

soups, pies, terrines and pâtés – dishes devised in the past to make use of small quantities of mixed game. Also included here are the time-honoured accompaniments to game such as game chips, fried breadcrumbs, rowan jelly and bread sauce.

I hope that this book will whet your appetite for foods you have not tried before as well as for those you have. We have a wealth of game in this country, both wild and farmed, and buying and cooking it has never been simpler.

FOOD SAFETY

Your game butcher takes the utmost care when storing and preparing game and game products to ensure that they are safe for you and your family. Once you have purchased your game, keep it safe by following these guidelines.

✦ Keep your kitchen clean. Always clean and disinfect equipment and working surfaces before food preparation and between the preparation of cooked and uncooked game.

✦ Always wash your hands thoroughly before and after handling any food and in between handling raw and cooked foods. If possible, use an antibacterial soap in the kitchen area.

✦ Keep cooked and raw game separate and covered. Store raw and cooked foods separately and uncooked foods lower in the fridge than cooked.

✦ Return leftover meats to the fridge as quickly as possible. Never allow the juices of raw meat and poultry to drip on to cooked foods.

✦ It is essential that you check your refrigerator on a regular basis to ensure that it is running at the right temperature, between 0°C and 4°C. Your freezer should be kept at minus 18°C or below.

✦ Do not reheat previously cooked game dishes more than once. Make sure they are reheated thoroughly.

✦ Frozen game must be thawed thoroughly before cooking, ideally at room temperature overnight. Do not re-freeze the game unless it has been cooked first.

GAME SEASONS

Blackcock	October–December	**Ptarmigan**	December–May
Duck	All year	**Quail**	June–August
Duck, wild	August–January	**Rabbit**	All year
Duckling	March–September	**Salmon**	February–October
Goose	September–March	**Snipe**	August–March
Gosling	March–September	**Teal**	September–March
Grouse	August–December	**Trout**	February–September
Guinea fowl	October–February	**Turkey**	All year
Hare	August–February	**Venison**	May–October
Partridge	September–February	**Wigeon**	August–March
Pheasant	October–February	**Wild boar**	All year
Pigeon	August–April	**Woodcock**	August–March

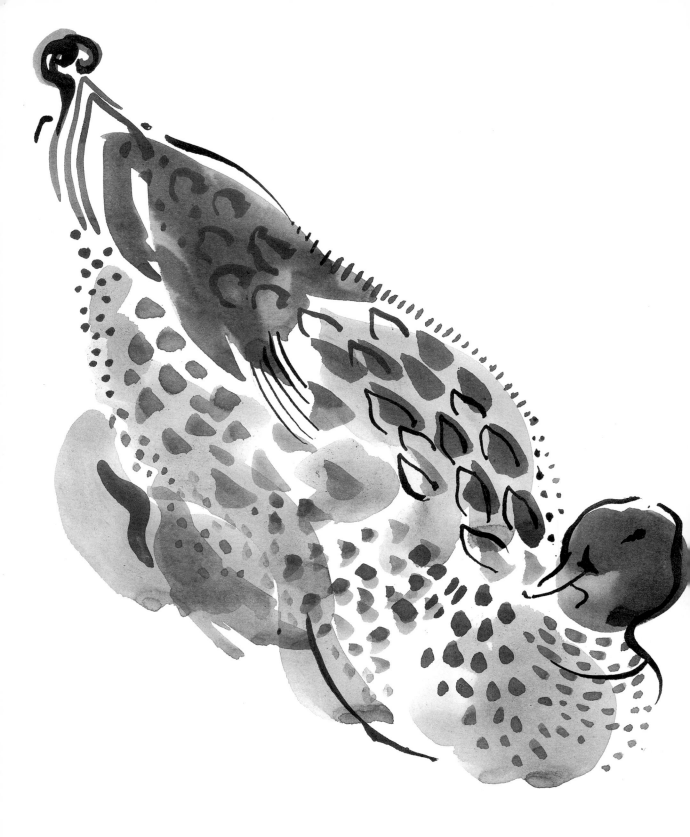

BIRDS OF A FEATHER

*G**ame birds come in all kinds of sizes and varieties, from the tiny quail to the majestic goose. In between these extremes come many well-known and popular birds such as the duck, pheasant, pigeon and grouse as well as those not so well known — the snipe, teal, wigeon and ptarmigan.*

Before any wild game bird can be cooked and eaten it must go through a procedure as old as game cookery itself, to make it ready for the oven. These days supermarkets and other suppliers provide game in oven-ready condition, but here is the procedure for those who either shoot their own game birds or buy them still feathered.

HANG 'EM HIGH

The flavour of most game birds is improved by hanging before plucking. During this hanging the flesh begins the process of decomposition, and the flavour is thereby accentuated. All game birds except pigeon and quail must be hung to bring out flavour, and also to make the game tender. Nowadays the hanging, plucking and drawing is mostly done for us by game suppliers, but I should still like to go through the process for readers who may have to do their own game preparation.

Game birds should be hung in their feathers in a cool place (not in a refrigerator) where the circulation of cold air can help the maturing and tenderizing of the meat. They should be hung by the neck and not the feet, and high enough to be out of the reach of dogs, cats, etc. When the feathers just above the tail come away easily, the birds are ready for plucking, but timing does depend on the weather and the condition of the bird. If a bird has not been cleanly shot, it can disintegrate very quickly and must be disposed of. If it was shot cleanly on a good clear day, it can hang for four days for pheasant, partridge or grouse, two days for wild duck. If it is raining and thundery, the game goes off quite quickly and needs to be plucked quickly.

PLUCKING

After a game bird has been hung it must be plucked. Put the bird inside a large plastic bag and start plucking the wings, keeping the feathers inside the bag. Then work from the neck to the tail, pulling the feathers away from the bird to avoid tearing the skin. Take extra care when plucking the breast.

Using a lit candle, singe any leftover tiny feathers from the bird, being very careful not to burn the skin.

DRAWING

You will need a sharp knife, a cutting board, kitchen paper, some salt and a sharp pair of kitchen scissors.

Place the cutting board on a firm working surface, then, with the sharp knife, cut off the bird's head at the top of the neck. Place the bird breast down on the cutting board, and with scissors cut down the neck, pulling away the loose skin. Pull out the windpipe and crop, removing the neck close to the spine.

With the knife make a short cut between the tail and the vent. Carefully push your fingers inside the bird, and, holding it firmly with the other hand, draw out the intestines, ensuring that the gizzard, liver, gall-bladder and heart are removed. Place the washed gizzard, liver, heart and neck into a saucepan with cold water and use this for your stock (page 142).

Wash the inside of the bird with cold salt water, and dry with kitchen paper. Season the inside again with salt, and place to one side for an hour.

JOINTING

Again a very sharp knife is required. Carefully cut the skin around the legs and body, pulling the legs outwards and apart and downwards so that the thighs open and break. Cut through the joint with the knife, separating the legs from the body. The legs can be left whole, or divided into drumsticks and thighs by cutting through the skin into the centre joint, breaking the centre joint open and cutting through with the knife.

Cut into the corners of the wings, taking a line from the breastbone downwards, which should include a slice of the breast meat. The breast is then separated from the back and cut in half lengthways. The jointed bird is now ready for cooking.

TRUSSING

You will need a trussing needle and some thin string. Should the bird need stuffing (page 149), this must be done before trussing. Place the stuffing in the loose skin from the neck, pressing it down into the body cavity of the bird. Carefully fold the skin from the neck under the back of the bird. The bird should now be breast side up. Fold the ends of the wings backwards and under to secure the loose skin. Firmly press the legs down into the sides.

Thread the trussing needle with the string.

Pass the needle through one wing joint, through the body, out at the top far leg, back on to the rear side, and tie the string firmly.

Thread the needle again and pass the string through the back of the bird, beneath the drumsticks, then carefully through both the drumsticks. Tie and secure. Your game bird is now trussed and ready for the oven.

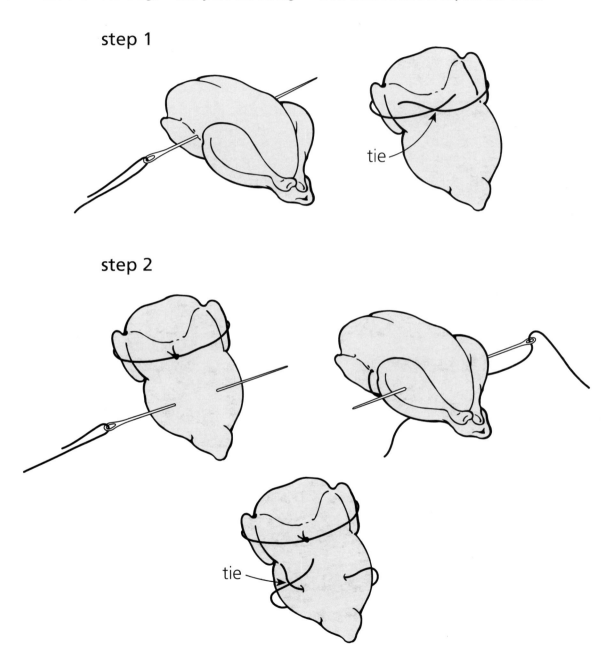

step 1

tie

step 2

tie

DUCK

There are two types of duck on the market: the wild duck and the domestic, farmed duck. It is the latter of these that people mean when they say (and I can't begin to count the number of times I have heard it): 'I don't like duck – it is far too greasy and fatty.' But the reason for this is quite simple: the duck has not been cooked properly. I believe it is the cook, and only the cook, who contributes to the success of a duck. The recipes that follow will help change a few minds about duck cookery.

DOMESTIC DUCK

There are several types of farmed duck available all year round in the UK, the main ones being Lincolnshire, Gressingham and Aylesbury. Lincolnshire ducks reach their prime at nine weeks, and weigh about 2.7kg (6lb). Gressingham, like the Aylesbury, have a thicker layer of skin than the Lincolnshire and therefore are fattier, as are the American Long Island or Pekin duck.

French ducks such as Barbary or Muscovy, and the Nantais and Rouen breeds, have far less fat and yield more meat than English ducks. The Barbary duck is large, and generously covered with meat, while the Nantais is smaller. The Rouen duck is unique to France, and resembles wild duck in taste and texture.

The weight of bone in a duck is high in proportion to the meat, and a large bird (about 2.5kg/5lb) is needed for 4 people. The Barbary can reach 4.5kg (10lb) and will serve 6–8. Boned duck breasts are sold separately as *magrets* and are usually cooked rare, while the legs can be preserved as *confit*.

Always check a bird for age by pressing its beak with your fingers. Young ducks have a flexible and quite soft beak; in older ducks the beak is hard and firm.

You never have to add fat to a farmed duck. A duck has so much fat it is self-basting. Cut off any visible fat before cooking and pour off excess fat as it accumulates in the roasting tin in the oven. (Save this fat, as it is ideal for roasting potatoes and parsnips to go with the Sunday roast.) Using a rack in the roasting tin is a prime way of allowing the fat to drip from the bird, preventing it sitting in its own fat and soaking it up again.

WILD DUCK

Wild ducks range in size from less than 500g (1lb) to 4.5kg (10lb) and can vary greatly in taste. They roast particularly well, and do not have nearly as much fat as domestic ducks.

The most common wild duck is the mallard, which is related to the domestic duck. Other members of the family sometimes available are teal, wigeon and pintail. Ducks that must not be killed are the Scaup duck, Garganey teal and long-tailed duck.

The season for wild duck runs from the end of August to the end of January. When choosing a wild duck, feel its feet and beak, which should be pliable and quite soft. Its age is vital, as birds over six months will need a slow method of cooking such as braising.

Roast Duckling

✦ **Serves 4** ✦

*I like to use Gressingham duck for this, and it is available at many good supermarkets.
It is tender, succulent in texture, and has a gamy flavour.*

1 x 2.7kg (6lb) Gressingham duckling	1 small onion, chopped
salt and freshly ground black pepper	1 apple, peeled, cored and chopped
juice of 1 lemon	2 tablespoons chopped celery leaves
1 garlic clove, halved	1 tablespoon sultanas
200ml (7fl oz) dry sherry	1 teaspoon freshly chopped sage
	150ml (5fl oz) freshly squeezed
FOR THE STUFFING	orange juice
4 tablespoons fresh breadcrumbs	

1 Preheat the oven to 180°C/350°F/gas 4.

2 Trim the wing tips of the duckling and cut off the neck. Remove any excess fat from the openings. Carefully wipe the inside and outside of the duckling with kitchen paper. Sprinkle the inside of the cavity with salt, pepper and the juice of the lemon.

3 Put the stuffing ingredients into a bowl and mix thoroughly. Push into the cavity, and truss the duckling.

4 Just before roasting, prick the skin of the duckling with a fork. Rub the cut clove of garlic over the breast, and season with salt and pepper. Place the duckling on a rack in a roasting tin, and roast in the centre of the preheated oven for 35 minutes. Remove the fat from the roasting tin, add the sherry and continue cooking, basting the duckling every 20 minutes, for the next 1¼ hours or so allowing 20 minutes per 450g (1lb).

5 Serve with gravy, fresh vegetables and noodles or game chips (page 149).

Breast of Gressingham Duckling Baked in Lemon Marmalade

✦ SERVES 4 ✦

This is a very British combination of tastes, as an excellent alternative to crispy Peking duck.
The duck breasts must be well pricked with a fork before cooking.

4 boneless Gressingham duck breasts	225g (8oz) shallots, sliced
salt and freshly ground black pepper	120ml (4fl oz) port
30ml (1fl oz) olive oil	30ml (1fl oz) brandy
25g (1oz) unsalted butter	1 tablespoon red wine vinegar
85g (3oz) thick-cut lemon marmalade	1 teaspoon pink peppercorns
85g (3oz) blackcurrants	

1 Preheat the oven to 230°C/450°F/gas 8.

2 Season the duck breasts and prick well with a fork or the point of a sharp knife. Heat the oil and butter in a frying pan. Seal the duck breasts over a high heat until lightly browned, then drain.

3 Put all the remaining ingredients into a bowl and mix thoroughly. Coat the breasts thickly with this marmalade mixture, then put them into a roasting tin. Bake in the oven for 20 minutes, basting every 5 minutes with the marmalade mixture.

4 Remove the duck breasts from the pan and slice each one into 8 slices lengthways. Keep them warm on a serving dish in the oven, turned to low.

5 Put the juices from the roasting tin into a saucepan and reduce over a high heat until of a thick sauce consistency. Pour over the slices of duck, put under a preheated hot grill for 1 minute, then serve.

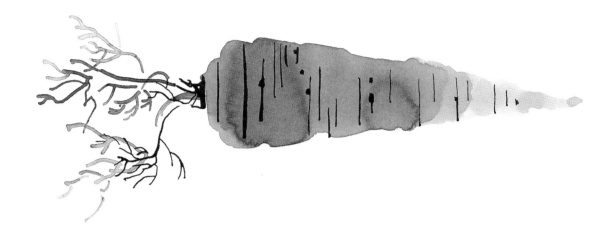

Julian Groom's Breast of Gressingham Duckling with Amaretto Sauce

✦ SERVES 4 ✦

A recipe from my friend Julian Groom of Le Meridian, Poona, India.

4 x 275g (10oz) boneless Gressingham duck breasts	150ml (5fl oz) chicken stock
salt and freshly ground black pepper	6 tablespoons Amaretto
25g (1oz) butter	100g (4oz) fresh or tinned black cherries
50g (2oz) finely chopped shallot	25g (1oz) plain flour
50g (2oz) finely chopped carrot	1 tablespoon Worcestershire sauce
1 tablespoon lemon juice	a handful of fresh cherries
	1 eating apple, cored and sliced

1 Trim the fat from the duck breasts, score the skin with a sharp knife, and season them well all over.

2 Melt the butter in a large frying pan, and seal the duck breasts for a few minutes on both sides.

3 Add the chopped shallot and carrot, the lemon juice and a little of the stock. Let simmer for 1 minute, then add the Amaretto and cherries and a sprinkling of flour. Allow to cook for a few minutes, then season with freshly ground black pepper and the Worcestershire sauce.

4 Remove the duck breasts from the pan, allowing the sauce to continue simmering. Slice the duck breasts lengthways into 5mm (¼ inch) pieces. Pour a little of the sauce on to each serving plate, then arrange the duck breasts in a fan shape on top. Garnish with fresh cherries and a slice of apple.

Peking Duckling

✦ SERVES 4 ✦

I was taught this recipe by one of the finest chefs in this country, David Lam, whose family have been in the restaurant and food business for nearly a century. This is my version, which should be served with mandarin pancakes, plum sauce (both available ready-made in good supermarkets), shredded leek, spring onion and cucumber. Yes, a hairdryer is needed to dry the duck. This will speed up the drying time by hours, and although the recipe sounds lengthy I assure you it will be well worth the time and effort.

1 × 2.3kg (5lb) Gressingham duckling	**TO SERVE**
3 tablespoons soy sauce	at least 16 mandarin pancakes
1 teaspoon salt	plum sauce
4 tablespoons clear honey	2 young leeks, shredded
1 tablespoon peeled and thinly sliced fresh ginger	8 spring onions, shredded
1 tablespoon white wine vinegar	½ cucumber, cut into fine strips
2 tablespoons dry sherry	

1 Wash the duckling thoroughly in hot water, then let it soak for 1 minute. This loosens the skin. Dry the duckling with kitchen paper thoroughly inside and out. Secure a piece of string around the duckling and hang it over a clean basin. Dry it thoroughly with the hairdryer.

2 Put the remaining ingredients in a saucepan. Bring to the boil then allow to cool.

3 Paint the duckling with the soy mixture, then dry again all over with the hairdryer for about 20 minutes. Repeat this process three times, then leave it to hang for 1½ hours (out of reach of dogs and cats).

4 Preheat the oven to 190°C/375°F/gas 5.

5 Place the duckling on a rack in a roasting tin and bake in the centre of the preheated oven for 1½ hours. *Do not open the oven until this time is complete.*

6 Allow the duckling to cool slightly, then shred the meat and skin off the bone. Serve with mandarin pancakes, plum sauce and shredded vegetables.

Chinese Egg Noodles with Duck

✦ SERVES **4** ✦

A quick and easy stir-fry that can be made using domestic or wild duck.

285g (10oz) Chinese egg noodles	340g (12oz) boneless duck breast, thinly sliced
3 tablespoons walnut oil	salt and freshly ground black pepper
2.5cm (1 inch) fresh ginger, cut into thin strips	1 tablespoon cornflour
5 spring onions, finely shredded	5 tablespoons dry sherry
2 garlic cloves, finely chopped	3 tablespoons soy sauce
1 red pepper, thinly sliced	1 teaspoon soft brown sugar
100g (4oz) button mushrooms, thinly sliced	225g (8oz) beansprouts
	1 tablespoon sesame oil

1 Bring 2.3 litres (4 pints) of water to the boil in a large saucepan and cook the noodles according to the packet instructions. Drain and set aside.

2 Heat the walnut oil in a wok. Stir in the ginger, spring onions and garlic and stir-fry for 45 seconds. Add the red pepper, mushrooms, sliced duck breast, salt and pepper, and stir-fry for 8 minutes. Mix the cornflour with the sherry and soy sauce and add to the pan with the brown sugar. Stir-fry for a further 4 minutes, then add the beansprouts, the drained noodles and the sesame oil. Stir and toss for 2 minutes, then serve.

Braised Drunken Duck

✦ SERVES 4 ✦

This recipe dates from the sixteenth century, but I have modernized it, and use Marsala, brandy and white wine to get the duck 'drunk'.

4 tablespoons olive oil	50ml (2fl oz) brandy
16 shallots, sliced	50ml (2fl oz) Marsala
3 garlic cloves, peeled and crushed	150ml (5fl oz) dry white wine
6 sprigs of fresh rosemary	50ml (2fl oz) apple juice
1 × 2.3kg (5lb) Gressingham duckling, cut into portions	1 large Bramley apple, peeled, cored and sliced
1 teaspoon coriander seeds, crushed	salt and freshly ground black pepper
1 tablespoon clear honey	

1 Preheat the oven to 170°C/325°F/gas 3.

2 Heat the olive oil in a large frying pan. Add the shallots, garlic and rosemary, and fry gently for 3 minutes. Add the duckling portions and fry for a further 5 minutes, until brown.

3 Pour the contents of the pan into a deep ovenproof casserole. Add the rest of the ingredients, season to taste, then cover with foil and braise in the oven for 1½ hours. Remove the foil and cook for a further 30 minutes uncovered.

4 Take out and discard the sprigs of rosemary and serve the drunken duck with a crisp salad, game chips (page 149) and a bottle of a good red such as Merlot del Vento.

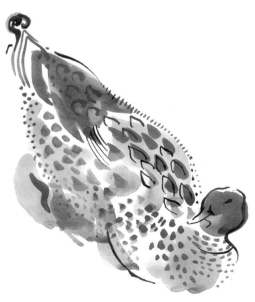

Crusty Baked Long Island Duck

✦ SERVES 4 ✦

The USA is famous for its Long Island ducklings, which are very plump and fat, giving this method of duck cookery the edge over any other. My cousin Lee lives there – I have yet to taste her cooking!

1 × 2.7kg (6lb) duckling with giblets	a pinch of freshly grated nutmeg
Game Stock (page 141)	a pinch of dried sage
salt and freshly ground black pepper	50g (2oz) fresh breadcrumbs
1 large egg	2 slices of bread
2 tablespoons fresh milk	a sprig of fresh sage

1 Remove all the skin from the duckling, with as much fat as possible. Put into a pan and cook over a low heat for 5 minutes. Remove the skin and keep fat and skin separate.

2 With a very sharp knife, cut out the backbone and neck of the duckling and place them in a saucepan with the giblets. Add enough game stock to cover, and season well with salt and pepper. Simmer for approximately 2 hours.

3 Meanwhile, divide the legs into thighs and drumsticks, remove the wings and divide the breast into 4 pieces. Remove any bones and add them to the stock.

4 Preheat the oven to 180°C/350°F/gas 4.

5 Beat the egg and milk together, then add the nutmeg and sage, and some salt and pepper. Carefully dip the duck pieces into the egg mixture, then toss them in the breadcrumbs. Brown them quickly in some of the heated rendered duck fat and transfer them to a casserole. Cover the casserole and bake in the centre of the preheated oven for 1 hour.

6 Cut both slices of bread into quarters and deep-fry them in hot duck fat. Serve the duck garnished with sage leaves and accompanied by the fried bread. Drink a crisp red Californian wine with it.

Wild Duckling with Oranges and Rose-Petal Vinegar

✦ **SERVES 4** ✦

This is a delightfully fresh-tasting dish, dedicated to Sue Webb and Icky.

25g (1oz) butter	50g (2oz) red peppers, cut into very fine strips
1 tablespoon olive oil	
4 × 225g (8oz) wild duckling suprêmes	50g (2oz) leeks, shredded
150ml (5fl oz) orange brandy	salt and freshly ground black pepper
150ml (5fl oz) rose-petal vinegar	3 fresh oranges, cut into segments, rind cut into very fine strips
15g (½oz) plain flour	
150ml (5fl oz) freshly squeezed orange juice	2 tablespoons chopped fresh tarragon
	150ml (5fl oz) fromage frais
50g (2oz) courgettes, cut into very fine strips	

1 Heat the butter and oil in a large frying pan, add the duck suprêmes, and cook slowly for 12 minutes until light golden brown all over. Remove from the pan and keep warm.

2 Add the orange brandy and rose-petal vinegar to the juices in the pan, and cook for a further 4 minutes. Sprinkle lightly with the flour, and cook for 5 minutes more. Reduce the heat and add the orange juice, courgettes, peppers and leeks. Season with salt and pepper, and simmer for 5 minutes, until the orange sauce is reduced and has thickened. Add half the orange segments, half the rind and half the tarragon plus all the fromage frais, and cook for a further 2 minutes.

3 Place each wild duck suprême in the centre of a warm plate, with a little sauce. Garnish with the remaining orange segments and tarragon leaves, and sprinkle with the remaining strips of orange rind. Serve with fresh noodles or on a bed of wild rice.

Roast Teal

The teal is the smallest member of the duck family, and has the best flavour. Its size makes it just right for one person. It is delicious simply roasted with nothing more than a little butter, but this recipe elaborates on the theme.

50g (2oz) butter	**6 oven-ready teal**
juice of 1 lemon	**12 rashers of streaky bacon**
225g (8oz) redcurrants or cranberries	**1 tablespoon thyme leaves**
salt and freshly ground black pepper	

1 Preheat the oven to 200°C/400°F/gas 6.

2 Gently melt the butter in a pan, add the lemon juice, the redcurrants or cranberries and a sprinkle of salt and pepper, and cook for 1 minute. Allow to cool.

3 Fill the cavity of each bird with the currant mixture, seasoning the birds well all over. Lay 2 slices of bacon over each breast. Sprinkle with thyme leaves.

4 Wrap each bird in greased foil and place breast down in a roasting tin. Roast for 15 minutes, then remove the foil and roast for a further 10 minutes.

5 Serve with bread sauce (page 147).

Teal Breasts in Creamed Brandy with Honey and Lemon

✦ SERVES **4** ✦

A different way to cook teal, in a delicious creamy but fresh-tasting sauce.

4 teal breasts	**150g (5oz) lemon slices**
50g (2oz) butter	**salt and freshly ground black pepper**
juice and zest of 2 lemons	**4 tablespoons brandy**
2 tablespoons clear honey	**150ml (5fl oz) sour cream or fromage frais**
1 tablespoon white wine vinegar	

1 Cut the teal breasts into thin slices.

2 Heat the butter in a frying pan, add the slices of teal and cook gently for 8 minutes, turning frequently until lightly coloured. Add the lemon juice, zest and honey and cook for a further 5 minutes.

3 Remove the teal slices from the pan and arrange around a large serving dish. Keep warm in a low oven.

4 Return the pan with the teal juices to the heat. Add the vinegar and lemon slices and simmer for 2 minutes. Season with salt and pepper, add the brandy, and cook for a further 3 minutes. Finally add the cream and simmer until reduced by half.

5 Remove the teal from the oven. Pour the sauce into the centre of the dish and serve immediately.

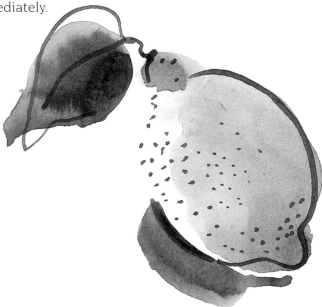

Duck Livers with Raspberry and Amaretto Sauce on a Bed of Bubble and Squeak Cakes

✦ SERVES 4 AS A STARTER ✦

This is one of my late dinner starters and looks wonderful served on a dark chocolate coloured plate. Drink a glass of Brut Champagne with it. You can also use chicken, goose or turkey livers for this recipe.

450g (1lb) fresh duck livers	**FOR THE BUBBLE AND SQUEAK CAKES**
50g (2oz) butter	60g (2½oz) duck fat
salt and freshly ground black pepper	1 medium onion, finely chopped
150ml (5fl oz) Amaretto	225g (8oz) cooked cabbage, finely chopped
2 tablespoons raspberry jelly	450g (1lb) potatoes, cooked and mashed
pinch of cayenne pepper	salt and freshly ground black pepper
2 tablespoons thick double cream	plain flour
100g (4oz) fresh raspberries	
1 sprig of fresh mint	

1 First make the bubble and squeak cakes. Heat 2 tablespoons of duck fat in a large frying pan. Add the chopped onion, cook for 3 minutes, then add the cabbage and cook for a further 3 minutes. Finally add the potatoes, season, and continue to cook over a medium heat for a further 10 minutes, stirring so that everything is well blended.

2 Remove the mixture to a bowl and allow to cool.

3 Flour a chopping board and your hands. Take about 50g (2oz) of the mixture at a time, roll into a ball and then flatten like a pancake. Heat the remaining duck fat and fry the cakes until golden brown, about 3 minutes either side. Keep them warm.

4 Remove the skin very carefully from the duck livers. Cut the livers into 4mm (¼ inch) thick slices.

5 Heat the butter in a frying pan and cook the livers quickly on each side. Sprinkle with salt and pepper. Remove them from the pan and keep them warm.

6 Pour away any excess fat from the pan, add the Amaretto and simmer for 2 minutes. Add the raspberry jelly, cayenne, cream and raspberries and simmer for 1 minute.

7 Place the bubble and squeak cakes on a large serving dish. Arrange the duck livers in a fan shape on top of the bubble and squeak cakes, pour the sauce around the cakes and garnish with a sprig of fresh mint.

PHEASANT

The pheasant is probably the best-known British game bird, recognizable by its beautiful plumage. It is thought of as a wild bird, but large numbers of pheasants are farmed and released into the wild by gamekeepers to increase the natural population.

Pheasant is available from the end of September to the end of January. Outside these times you can buy it frozen. In November and December the bird will be at its best. I prefer to cook a young hen rather than a cock pheasant, because it will generally be a good deal more tender and its flesh will be more succulent and moist.

When choosing a pheasant, feel the breastbone and beak, which should be flexible. The spurs on the feet should not be too pronounced, the feathers should be dry, and the eyes should be clear and not sunken.

Pheasant is a very healthy meat, low in fat and cholesterol and high in protein. It has a gamy flavour which will vary in strength depending on how long the bird has been hung – anything from 3–12 days according to the age of the bird and the season. A pheasant bought in a supermarket will probably taste much milder than one bought from a specialist butcher.

Pheasant lends itself to all kinds of recipes, but in general a young bird is best for quick cooking such as roasting or grilling. Older birds are good casseroled. The following recipes can also be used with grouse, ptarmigan and blackcock.

Roast Pheasant with Calvados and Apples

✦ SERVES 2 ✦

The flavours of France – a delicious recipe given to me several years ago by my friend David Hinds.

1 garlic clove	**4 tablespoons Calvados**
½ teaspoon salt	**1 large oven-ready pheasant**
1 teaspoon freshly ground black pepper	**4 baking apples, cored and peeled**
4 tablespoons lemon juice	**extra Calvados to serve**
4 tablespoons olive oil	

1 Blend the garlic, salt, pepper, lemon juice, oil and Calvados in a pestle and mortar or a liquidizer. Refrigerate the mixture for 4 hours to allow the flavours to mature.

2 Preheat the oven to 200°C/400°F/gas 6.

3 Put the pheasant in a roasting tin and coat generously with the Calvados mixture. Grind fresh black pepper over the pheasant, put the tin in the lower part of the oven and cook for about 60 minutes, basting every 20 minutes with the coating. During the last 30 minutes add the apples to the roasting tin.

4 Put the pheasant on a large serving dish. Garnish with the sliced apples, sprinkle with a little more Calvados and serve.

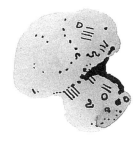

Roast Pheasant Breasts in Coriander Cream

✦ SERVES 4 ✦

This dish can also be made using grouse or wood pigeon instead of pheasant.
The coriander gives a lovely fresh taste.

75g (3oz) butter, softened	12 shallots
1 garlic clove, crushed	5 tablespoons chopped fresh coriander
salt and freshly ground black pepper	25g (1oz) plain flour
4 pheasant breasts	150ml (5fl oz) brandy
25g (1oz) dripping	300ml (10fl oz) double cream
175g (6oz) baby button mushrooms	

1 Place the butter, crushed garlic, salt and pepper in a bowl. Generously rub the mixture over the pheasant breasts and leave for 24 hours, covered, in a cool place.

2 Preheat the oven to 230°C/450°F/gas 8.

3 Heat the dripping in a large roasting tin and quickly brown the pheasant all over. Bake in the centre of the oven for 40 minutes, basting every 10 minutes. Take the pheasant breasts from the roasting tin and allow them to cool slightly on a wire rack.

4 Pour the juices from the roasting tin into a saucepan and cook the mushrooms, shallots and 4 tablespoons of coriander for 5 minutes. Sprinkle with the flour. Warm the brandy, add to the pan and ignite, then add the cream and cook for 3 minutes on a very low heat, stirring all the time.

5 Put the pheasant breasts into a casserole dish, cover with the cream sauce and bake in the oven for a further 12 minutes on 170°C/325°F/gas 3. Serve sprinkled with the remaining coriander.

Festive Mustard Baked Pheasant

✦ SERVES 4 ✦

This is a recipe I developed for the BBC Good Food Show in Birmingham. Pheasant and mustard go together like beef and horseradish, or peaches and cream – the perfect combination. You can also use guinea fowl, grouse or wood pigeon.

8 pheasant joints	1 tablespoon brown sugar
50g (2oz) butter, softened	1 teaspoon paprika
4 tablespoons mild mustard	salt and freshly ground black pepper
2 tablespoons lemon juice	3 tablespoons poppy seeds

1 Preheat the oven to 200°C/400°F/gas 6.

2 Place the pheasant joints in a large ovenproof dish. Put all the remaining ingredients except the poppy seeds into a large bowl and mix thoroughly. Using a pastry brush, paint the mixture on to the surface of the pheasant pieces. Bake in the centre of the oven for 15 minutes.

3 Carefully turn over the pheasant pieces, spooning the mixture over the pheasant. Sprinkle with the poppy seeds and return to the oven for a further 15 minutes.

4 Arrange the pheasant on a serving dish, pour over the juices and serve with a fresh crisp salad.

Pheasant with Baby Onions and Green Peas

✦ SERVES 4 ✦

225g (8oz) pork fat, diced	salt and freshly ground black pepper
50g (2oz) butter	1 bouquet garni
16 small onions or shallots	450g (1lb) fresh peas
2 large oven-ready pheasants	1 tablespoon honey
25g (1oz) plain flour	
600ml (20fl oz) Game Stock (page 141)	
or chicken stock	

1 Preheat the oven to 200°C/400°F/gas 6.

2 Put the pork fat cubes into a pan of boiling salted water. Simmer for 3 minutes, drain and dry.

3 Melt the butter in a large frying pan, add the pork and onions and cook for 3 minutes until lightly browned. Remove the pork and onions from the pan, put in the pheasants and brown them all over. Remove the pheasants from the pan and place in a roasting tin.

4 Add the flour to the pan, cook until it begins to brown, then slowly blend in the stock. Season with salt and pepper.

5 Pour the sauce over the pheasants, add the bouquet garni, and cook in the preheated oven for 45 minutes. Ten minutes before the end of the cooking time, remove the bouquet garni and add the onions, pork, peas and honey.

6 Serve the pheasants on a large serving dish, surrounded with the pork, peas, onions and gravy.

Sussex Houghed Pheasant and Grouse Breasts with Smoked Bacon

✦ Serves 4 ✦

The word 'hough' or 'huffed' means 'wrapped in a blanket' — i.e. wrapped in pastry, a very old method used by Elizabeth Raffald in 1769. This is a version of a famous north-country recipe called 'Hindle Wakes'.

4 × 175g (6oz) pheasant breasts	1 large onion, chopped
4 × 175g (6oz) grouse breasts	100g (4oz) dried prunes, stoned
8 rashers of rindless smoked bacon	and chopped
450g (1lb) suet crust pastry (page153)	50g (2oz) fresh white breadcrumbs
Sauce Chasseur (page 144), to serve	1 tablespoon port
	salt and freshly ground black pepper
For the Filling	1 large egg, beaten
100g (4oz) apple, peeled, cored and chopped	

1 Preheat the oven to 200°C/400°F/gas 6.

2 Put all the filling ingredients into a bowl, reserving a little of the egg, and mix thoroughly. Make a small pocket in each pheasant and grouse breast and fill generously with the mixture.

3 Place each pheasant breast on top of a grouse breast and secure with 2 pieces of smoked bacon.

4 Roll out the pastry on a floured board. Divide the pastry into 4 and wrap the pastry around each pheasant and grouse breast. Brush the top of the pastry with the reserved beaten egg. Place on a lightly greased baking sheet and bake in the centre of the oven for 30–35 minutes.

5 Serve with Sauce Chasseur.

Pheasant and Blackcock Casserole with Wild Mushrooms and Shallots

✦ **SERVES 4** ✦

One of my favourite non-profit-making organizations is the Game Marketing Executive, whose aim is quite simple – to get Britain eating game. My friend Louisa Ayland, who works there, gave me this wonderful recipe. I have made a small adaptation, adding honey and a little rosemary.

1 pheasant, jointed	2 bay leaves
1 blackcock, jointed	290ml (10fl oz) claret
25g (1oz) plain flour, well seasoned	425ml (15fl oz) chicken stock
50g (2oz) butter	1 tablespoon honey
50ml (2fl oz) olive oil	225g (8oz) shallots
8 sprigs of thyme	225g (8oz) wild mushrooms, sliced
4 sprigs of rosemary	salt and freshly ground black pepper
6 juniper berries	

1 Preheat the oven to 190°C/375°F/gas 5.

2 Toss the pheasant and blackcock joints in the seasoned flour. Heat the butter and oil in a deep flameproof casserole, and gently fry the meat all over until lightly browned. Add the remaining flour, the thyme, rosemary, juniper berries and bay leaves, and cook for a further 3 minutes. Slowly add the claret and chicken stock and simmer for 10 minutes.

3 Add the honey, shallots and mushrooms and season with salt and pepper. Cover with a lid or cooking foil and cook in the centre of the oven for 1 hour. Remove the thyme, rosemary and bay leaves and serve with pasta or noodles.

Wholemeal Spaghetti with Suprême of Pheasant

✦ SERVES **4** ✦

Try to get wholemeal spaghetti for this dish — it complements the pheasant beautifully.

25ml (1fl oz) vegetable oil	50g (2oz) leeks, finely shredded
1 tablespoon olive oil	salt and freshly ground black pepper
8 pheasant suprêmes	400g (14oz) wholemeal spaghetti
150ml (5fl oz) orange brandy	3 large fresh oranges, cut into segments
15g (½oz) plain flour	rind of 1 orange, cut into very fine strips
150ml (5fl oz) freshly squeezed	2 tablespoons freshly chopped tarragon
orange juice	150ml (5fl oz) fromage frais
50g (2oz) courgettes, cut into fine strips	whole tarragon leaves to garnish
50g (2oz) red peppers, cut into fine strips	

1 Heat the oils in a large frying pan. Add the pheasant suprêmes and cook quickly until a light golden brown. Add the orange brandy and cook for a further 3 minutes, then sprinkle lightly with the flour and cook for a further 2 minutes.

2 Reduce the heat and add the orange juice, courgettes, peppers and leeks. Season with salt and pepper and simmer for 5 minutes until the sauce reduces and thickens.

3 Meanwhile cook the pasta for 10 minutes or until *al dente*, and drain. Put the pasta on a warm large serving dish, sprinkle with a little olive oil, and keep warm.

4 Add half the orange segments and rind to the sauce. Stir in the tarragon and fromage frais and cook for a further 3 minutes.

5 Arrange the pheasant suprêmes on top of the pasta and pour over a little of the orange sauce. Serve garnished with the remaining orange segments and sprinkled with fresh tarragon leaves and the remaining orange rind.

PARTRIDGE

There are two types of partridge: the English or grey, and the red-legged or French. The grey partridge is found throughout the UK, and the red-legged partridge particularly in the south.

The partridge is considered by some to be the 'king of game birds', and many people prefer it to pheasant. It is in season from the beginning of September to the end of January, and is a low-fat, low-cholesterol meat.

Partridge should be hung for 3–5 days. The legs should be smooth and the breastbone pliable. It can be cooked like pheasant, but my preference is for roasting. Partridges can also be roasted wrapped in vine leaves – baste every 10 minutes and serve on a bed of saffron rice.

Roast Partridge

✦ SERVES 4 ✦

This is the best way to cook very young partridge.

4 young partridges	salt and freshly ground black pepper
duck fat	8 rashers rindless streaky bacon

1 Rub the birds with duck fat and season well with salt and pepper. Lay the bacon rashers over each breast.

2 Preheat the oven to 200°C/400°F/gas 6. Place the partridges in a roasting tin just large enough to take the birds, cover with foil and cook in the preheated oven for 45 minutes, removing the foil towards the end of the cooking time.

Grilled Partridge

✦ SERVES 4 ✦

Use only tender young partridges for grilling. They can be cooked under a very hot grill, or on a barbecue.

1 Split 4 partridges down the back, forcing the halves apart until they are completely flat.

2 Mix together 25g (1oz) of butter, 1 tablespoon of extra virgin olive oil, 1 teaspoon of lemon juice, salt and freshly ground black pepper, and use this mixture to baste the partridges.

3 Grill for 15 minutes, basting and turning them every 3 minutes.

Roast Partridge in Chive and Brandy Cream

✦ SERVES 4 ✦

This recipe is time-consuming but well worth it. For Kevin O'Sullivan at Fairfax Meadow.

75g (3oz) butter, softened	12 shallots, sliced
2 garlic cloves, crushed	25g (1oz) seasoned plain flour
2 tablespoons freshly snipped chives	150ml (5fl oz) brandy
salt and freshly ground black pepper	150ml (5fl oz) Espagnole Sauce (page143)
4 partridges	150ml (5fl oz) double cream
25g (1oz) butter	3 tablespoons freshly snipped chives
175g (6oz) button mushrooms, sliced	1 tablespoon freshly chopped parsley

1 Mix the softened butter, crushed garlic, chives, salt and pepper in a bowl. Generously rub the mixture over the partridges, inside and out, and leave for 24 hours, covered, in a cool place.

2 Preheat the oven to 220°C/425°F/gas 7. Heat the butter in a large roasting tin and quickly brown the partridges all over. Bake in the centre of the oven for 30 minutes, basting every 10 minutes. Take the partridges from the roasting tin and allow them to cool slightly on a wire rack.

3 Pour the juices into a saucepan, add the mushrooms and shallots, and cook for 5 minutes. Sprinkle with the flour. Warm the brandy, add it to the pan and ignite, then add the Espagnole sauce and cook for 5 minutes. Stir in the cream and cook for 4 minutes on a very low heat, stirring all the time.

4 Carefully cut the partridges into quarters, removing as many bones as you can. Place the partridge quarters in a casserole dish, cover with the cream sauce and bake in the oven for a further 12 minutes at 170°C/325°F/gas 3. Sprinkle with the chives and parsley.

Partridge Suprêmes Princess Royal

✦ **SERVES 4** ✦

I have had the privilege of cooking for and meeting HRH The Princess Royal on several occasions, and have great admiration for her hard work with the Save the Children Fund.

8 partridge suprêmes, bone left in, trimmed	16 slices of truffle
100g (4oz) rindless smoked bacon	salt and freshly ground black pepper
8 very thin slices of York ham	150ml (5fl oz) Madeira Sauce (page 145)
8 thin slices of sun-dried tomato	truffle shavings

1 Place each suprême between two sheets of clingfilm and flatten with a rolling pin until nearly transparent.

2 Put each suprême on a slice of bacon and top with a slice of York ham, a piece of sun-dried tomato and 2 slices of truffle. Season well with salt and pepper.

3 Fold the pointed end of the suprême over the truffle and then fold over again to form a parcel. Wrap each parcel in a large piece of clingfilm and either steam them for 14 minutes or poach them in boiling water. Meanwhile make up the Madeira sauce.

4 Remove the clingfilm from the partridge and cut the suprêmes into neat thin slices with a very sharp knife. Arrange the slices on a warm serving dish, pour the sauce around the edge of the partridge slices and garnish with truffle shavings.

Suprêmes of Partridge Filled with Lobster

✦ Serves 6 ✦

Louisa, my friend from the Game Marketing Executive, tried this at the BBC Good Food Show and declared it simply delightful.

6 partridge breasts

For the filling
100g (4oz) lobster meat
2 shallots, minced

2 fresh or dried figs, chopped
1 tablespoon Marsala
2 tablespoons fresh breadcrumbs
salt and freshly ground black pepper
1 large egg, beaten

1 Preheat the oven to 200°C/400°F/gas 6.

2 Place all the filling ingredients in a bowl and mix them thoroughly.

3 Make a small pocket in each partridge breast and fill generously with the mixture.

4 Wrap the partridge breasts in buttered foil, place them on a lightly greased baking sheet, and bake in the centre of the preheated oven for 35 minutes. Carefully remove the foil, slice the breasts very thinly, and serve with noodles.

Braised Breast of Partridge Filled with Wild Boar Sausage and Mushrooms

✦ SERVES 4 ✦

The wild boar sausagemeat works beautifully with the partridges in this recipe. The result is a wonderfully rich dish, perfect for entertaining.

8 partridge breasts	150ml (5fl oz) Espagnole Sauce (page 143)
450g (1lb) wild boar sausagemeat	2 tablespoons brandy
225g (8oz) mushrooms, chopped	1 tablespoon Rowan Jelly (page 146)
salt and freshly ground black pepper	24 shallots
225g (8oz) rindless streaky bacon	

1 Preheat the oven to 200°C/400°F/gas 6.

2 Cut a long slit horizontally along each partridge breast to make a pocket shape. Insert equal amounts of sausagemeat and chopped mushrooms, and season lightly. Carefully wrap enough bacon around each breast to cover completely the pocket containing the meat and mushrooms.

3 Place the breasts into an ovenproof casserole dish, pour over the Espagnole sauce and brandy, and add the rowan jelly and shallots. Cover with a lid or cooking foil and braise in the preheated oven for 30 minutes. Carefully remove the partridge breasts to a chopping board and slice them partially through to make a fan effect. Put them on a warm serving dish and garnish with the shallots.

4 Pour the juices from the casserole into a saucepan, bring to the boil and reduce by half. Serve with the partridge.

Rigatoni and Pesto Baked Partridge

✦ **Serves 4** ✦

These days you can buy good pesto sauce in jars at the supermarket or delicatessen.

8 partridge joints	1 teaspoon paprika
50g (2oz) butter, softened	salt and freshly ground black pepper
4 tablespoons mild mustard	6 tablespoons bought pesto sauce
2 tablespoons lemon juice	450g (1lb) rigatoni
1 tablespoon brown sugar	100g (4oz) freshly grated Parmesan cheese

1 Preheat the oven to 200°C/400°F/gas 6.

2 Put the partridge joints in a large ovenproof dish.

3 Put the butter, mustard, lemon juice, sugar, paprika, salt and pepper into a large bowl and blend the ingredients thoroughly. Using a pastry brush, paint the mixture on to the partridge joints.

4 Bake the partridge joints in the centre of the preheated oven for 15 minutes, then remove them from the oven, coat them with 3 tablespoons of pesto sauce, and return them to the oven for a further 12 minutes. Carefully turn over the partridge joints, spoon over the juices, and return them to the oven for a further 10 minutes.

5 Meanwhile cook the pasta for 10 minutes or until *al dente*. Drain the pasta and place in a large serving dish. Stir in the remaining pesto and the Parmesan. Arrange the pieces of partridge on top, pour over the juices and serve.

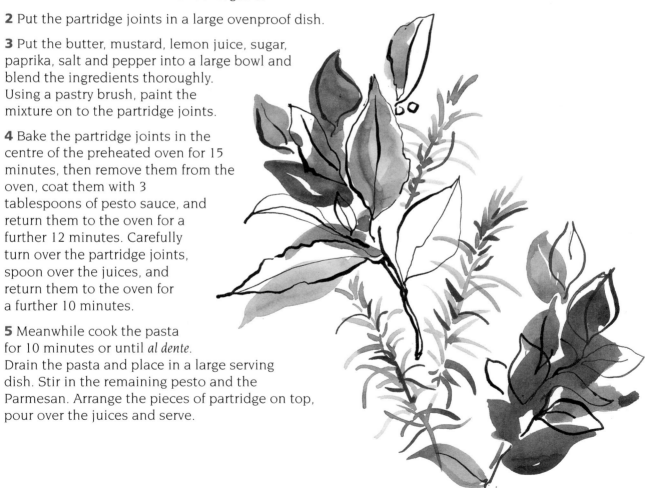

QUAIL

The quail is a small game bird related to the partridge. It originated in the eastern Mediterranean, and over the centuries it has become highly prized for its sporting and culinary qualities. Although classified as game in its natural environment, the British climate cannot sustain quail in the wild. These delicious birds have been reared in the UK for many years, and can be bought fresh at any time. Quail is available in many supermarkets and by mail order.

Owing to its unique size and light, delicate flavour, quail can be used in a variety of dishes both as a main course and as a starter. It has long been a favourite with chefs and restaurateurs, bringing a touch of variety and originality to the table. It is easy to prepare, extremely versatile, delicious to eat and very good value for money.

My favourite historical character is Rosa Lewis, the Queen of Cooks, who inspired the television series *The Duchess of Duke Street*. Her favourite game bird was quail, and her favourite recipe was Quail Pudding. Rosa worked with Soyer and Escoffier, and cooked for the King of England, the Kaiser, the lords, ladies, dukes, earls and all the greats of the early twentieth century at the Cavendish Hotel in St. James's, London. In the early 1990s I met Julian Groom, then general manager of the Cavendish, who was to become a very dear friend and colleague, and I was privileged to look at the original Cavendish menus. Each one had a different quail dish. I decided to recreate those wonderful recipes, and here are some of my favourites.

Joan Whittle's Quail with Mushrooms

✦ SERVES 4–8 ✦

This recipe is adapted from one given to Joan by chef Serge Pitarch, from Nîmes. Joan is a leading food consultant from the North of England.

2 tablespoons olive oil	8 garlic cloves, unpeeled
8 oven-ready quails	225g (8oz) button mushrooms, sliced
2 slices of streaky bacon	salt and freshly ground black pepper
300ml (½ pint) Madeira	4 slices of toast, cut in half
2 bay leaves	

1 Preheat the oven to 190°C/375°F/gas 5.

2 Heat the olive oil in a large flameproof casserole. Brown the quails, add the bacon and cook for 2 minutes. Stir in the Madeira, bay leaves and garlic.

3 Cover the casserole and cook in the preheated oven for 45–50 minutes, turning the quails after 30 minutes and adding the mushrooms.

4 Put the cooked quails on a warm serving dish. Transfer the cooking liquid to a small saucepan, bring to the boil and simmer until reduced by a quarter. Taste and season.

5 To serve, place a quail and a garlic clove on each half slice of toast, and serve the sauce in a sauceboat.

Rosa's Honey Roast Quail with Mint and Garlic

✦ Serves 4 ✦

Quail was a favourite of the Prince of Wales on his visits to the Duchess of Duke Street's residence, where the champagne flowed like water. Rosa Lewis was a duchess in the eyes not just of the Prince of Wales, but of everyone who frequented her restaurant, including the great Escoffier. This recipe is dedicated to Dee Ludlow.

8 boneless oven-ready quails	**8 garlic cloves**
freshly ground black pepper	**1 teaspoon salt**
	2 teaspoons freshly ground black pepper
For the coating	**8 tablespoons lemon juice**
4 tablespoons honey	**8 tablespoons olive oil**
8 sprigs of fresh mint	

1 Grind all the ingredients for the coating in a pestle and mortar, or blend them thoroughly in a liquidizer. Put the mixture into the refrigerator for 4 hours to allow the flavours to mature.

2 Preheat the oven to 200°C/400°F/gas 6.

3 Put the quails into a roasting tin and spread generously with the coating. Grind fresh black pepper over the quails, and cook in the lower part of the preheated oven for about 30 minutes, basting every 10 minutes.

4 Serve the quails with baked potatoes with sour cream and chives.

Variations

✦ Coat the quail with your favourite herb butter and roast at 200°C/400°F/gas 6 for 25 minutes, basting with the butter. Allow to cool slightly and serve warm with a fresh asparagus salad and a home-made garlic mayonnaise.

✦ Wrap each quail in bacon and roast for 25 minutes, basting with butter. Serve on croûtes of fried bread.

✦ Marinate the quail in a large deep tray at room temperature for 6 hours, with 6 tablespoons each of sherry, soy sauce and sesame oil, 1 tablespoon of chopped fresh ginger, 1 grated nutmeg, salt and freshly ground black pepper, then roast for 25 minutes.

David Niven's Cailles Rôties sur Canapés

✦ SERVES 4 ✦

This was a favourite dish of the actor David Niven, for whom I was privileged to create and cook it at a dinner organized in Portugal in the early Seventies.

extra virgin olive oil	24 shallots
12 slices of white bread, crusts removed	12 tablespoons crushed walnuts
100g (4oz) melted butter	190ml (7fl oz) port
12 × 150g (5oz) oven-ready quails, with livers	24 mint leaves
salt and freshly ground black pepper	24 slices of rindless smoked streaky bacon
3 garlic cloves, crushed	soft-boiled quail eggs, to garnish
24 juniper berries	(see below)

1 Preheat the oven to 230°C/450°F/gas 8.

2 Lightly brush a large ovenproof dish with extra virgin olive oil and carefully place the slices of bread into the dish. Sprinkle each slice lightly with melted butter.

3 Season the inside and outside of each quail with salt and pepper.

4 Place the garlic, juniper berries, shallots and walnuts into a saucepan with the port and heat gently for 15 minutes, then increase the heat and cook until the liquid is completely evaporated. Spoon equal amounts of the walnut mixture inside each quail.

5 Place 2 mint leaves on to each quail and wrap each with 2 slices of bacon. Tie the quails with butcher's string. Arrange them on the buttered bread and roast in the preheated oven for 10 minutes, then remove the bacon, reduce the heat to 200°C/400°F/gas 6 and roast for a further 15 minutes. Remove the dish from the oven, remove the string from the quails and serve with the bacon, finely chopped, and garnished with soft-boiled quail eggs.

Quail Eggs

Quail eggs with their beautiful speckled shells are ideal for garnishing any of the recipes in this book. They come in cartons of 12 and can now be found in the larger supermarkets and also in good butchers and fishmongers. Put the eggs into a pan with cold water and bring to the boil. Simmer for 2 minutes for soft-boiled, 3–4 minutes for hard-boiled, then plunge them into cold water.

Cailles aux Raisins

✦ **SERVES 4** ✦

Quails and grapes are a wonderful combination.

8 slices of rindless smoked back bacon	1 teaspoon cornflour
8 oven-ready quails	1 nutmeg
50g (2oz) butter	8 tablespoons sesame oil
salt and freshly ground black pepper	8 slices of white bread, crusts removed
4 tablespoons brandy	60ml (2floz) grape juice
450g (1lb) seedless black and white grapes	

1 Wrap a slice of bacon around each quail and tie with butcher's string. Melt half the butter in a large frying pan and brown the quails quickly. Remove the quails from the pan, pour away the excess fat and wipe the pan with kitchen paper. Season the pan with salt and freshly ground black pepper and add the remaining butter. When it has melted add the quails and the brandy, cover the pan and leave to one side for 30 minutes so that the alcohol can flavour the birds.

2 Meanwhile crush half the grapes and blend the juice with the cornflour. Cut the remaining grapes into quarters and reserve.

3 Put the pan back on the heat, adding the grape juice and cornflour to the liquid. Grate the nutmeg over the quails and simmer for 20 minutes.

4 Heat the sesame oil in a separate frying pan and fry the slices of bread until golden brown. Put the fried bread on a large serving plate and arrange the quartered grapes on top. Remove the string from the quails and place a quail on each bread slice. Serve with the grape sauce and game chips (page 149).

Variations

You can repeat this recipe using grape juice, orange juice and apple juice and adding 450g (1lb) of the fruit either cut into segments or finely diced.

Quail Peking Style

✦ SERVES 4 ✦

A variation on the famous Peking duck.

12 oven-ready quails	1 tablespoon thinly sliced fresh ginger
4 tablespoons soy sauce	1 tablespoon white wine vinegar
1 teaspoon salt	2 tablespoons dry sherry
4 tablespoons clear honey	

1 Dry the quails inside and out with kitchen paper. Tie a piece of string around each quail and hang up by the string over a clean basin. Dry each quail thoroughly, using a hairdryer.

2 Place the soy sauce, salt, honey, ginger, vinegar and sherry in a saucepan, bring to the boil and then allow to cool. Paint the quails all over with the soy sauce mixture and dry with the hairdryer for 5 minutes. Repeat this process 3 times and then leave the quails to hang for 30 minutes.

3 Preheat the oven to 190°C/375°F/gas 5. Place the quails on a rack in a roasting tin and bake in the centre of the preheated oven for 30 minutes. Do not attempt to open the oven until the 30 minutes is up.

4 Allow the quails to cool slightly and serve them with plum sauce and some egg fried rice.

Rosa's Quail Pudding

✦ SERVES 4 ✦

Rosa Lewis, the inspiration for the television series The Duchess of Duke Street, *was chef/proprietor of one of my favourite London hotels, the Cavendish. Rosa was famous for her game sauces, pies and quail recipes, especially her famous Quail Pudding, created for her long-time friend Edward VII. Rosa also made her pudding for White's, one of London's oldest gentlemen's clubs. If you don't want to spend time steaming the pudding, serve the quail meat sliced with vegetables and serve the sauce in a sauceboat. You can use breast meat from other game birds.*

50g (2oz) butter	100g (4oz) shallots, sliced
a pinch of fines herbes	150ml (5fl oz) fresh orange juice
12 quail breasts, skin removed, thinly sliced	1 sprig of fresh thyme
6 slices of rindless smoked streaky bacon, diced	4 tablespoons brandy
	salt and freshly ground black pepper
12 × 25g (1oz) slices of sirloin of beef	150ml (5fl oz) Espagnole Sauce (page 143)
100g (4oz) button mushrooms	225g (8oz) Suet Pastry (page153)

1 Melt the butter in a large frying pan. Add the herbs, quail, bacon, beef, mushrooms and shallots, and fry them for 6 minutes.

2 Add the orange juice, thyme, brandy and seasoning to the pan, and simmer for at least 20 minutes until the liquid is reduced by half.

3 Add the Espagnole sauce and simmer until reduced by half again. Butter a 30-cm (12-inch) pudding basin and line it with suet pastry. Fill with the meat and game sauce. Cover the top of the basin with a suet pastry lid and seal. Gently brush the top with melted butter and cover with several layers of cooking foil. Steam the pudding in a covered saucepan for 3 hours, topping up the pan with extra water as necessary.

Quail and Rabbit Casserole

✦ SERVES 4 ✦

I created this dish for a very royal personage during a visit to Portugal several years ago. You can use virtually any game for this recipe, but quail must always be included to get the right mildness.

50g (2oz) butter	1 leek, sliced
2 tablespoons olive oil	1 parsnip, diced
450g (1lb) boneless quail meat, chopped	100g (4oz) mushrooms, quartered
450g (1lb) boneless rabbit meat, chopped	4 tablespoons sweet sherry
50g (2oz) seasoned flour	1 teaspoon dried basil
100g (4oz) rindless streaky bacon	1 tablespoon crushed rosemary
4 potatoes, chopped	6 crushed juniper berries
3 onions, sliced	salt and freshly ground black pepper
2 carrots, sliced	600ml (1 pint) Espagnole Sauce (page 143)

1 Preheat the oven to 170°C/325°F/gas 3.

2 Heat the butter and oil in a large casserole. Toss the meats into the seasoned flour and cook quickly for 4 minutes, sealing all the juices into the game. Trim the bacon, cutting each rasher into 5 or 6 pieces, and add to the casserole with the vegetables and the sherry. Sprinkle with the herbs and juniper berries and season well. Pour over the Espagnole sauce. Simmer for 5 minutes, then cover the casserole and cook in the centre of the preheated oven for 2 hours.

Prelice sa Pirincem (Quail in a Coconut Curry Sauce)

✦ **SERVES 6–8** ✦

*Slovenia, where this recipe originates, is a very rich game hunting area, and wild quail
are considered among its finest game birds. You can use any mild game meat.*

900g (2lb) quail meat
50g (2oz) grated coconut
300ml (10fl oz) coconut cream
½ teaspoon garam masala

FOR THE COCONUT CURRY PASTE
6 garlic cloves
2.5cm (1 inch) fresh ginger, peeled
and coarsely chopped
50g (2oz) blanched almonds
6 tablespoons Game Stock (page 000)
1 teaspoon ground cardamom

2 tablespoons grated coconut
4 tablespoons coconut cream
4 cloves, crushed
1 teaspoon soft brown sugar
1 teaspoon cinnamon
2 large onions, chopped
1 teaspoon coriander seeds, crushed
2 teaspoons cumin seeds, crushed
pinch of cayenne
salt and freshly ground black pepper
6 tablespoons olive oil

1 Place all the ingredients for the curry paste into a liquidizer, and blend the ingredients thoroughly together until very smooth. Coat the quail with the curry mixture and place in the refrigerator for 3 hours.

2 Put the meat and its marinade into a large saucepan. Simmer gently for 35 minutes, adding a little game stock if required. Add the grated coconut, coconut cream and garam masala and simmer for a further 30 minutes.

3 Allow the curry to stand for 10 minutes before serving with saffron rice.

PIGEON

In the Middle Ages in England every house of importance had its dovecot, and many old English pigeon recipes date back to that time. In the eighteenth century pigeons were still very popular and became a characteristic of English cookery.

Despite being one of the smallest and cheapest of game birds, pigeons are delicious. They are available all year round but are at their best between May and October. They are sold both whole and as breast fillets, though the latter are more expensive. It is better to buy the whole bird, cut off the breasts and use the rest to make a good game stock (page 141).

A simple method of roasting or grilling pigeon is to smear it with herb butter, season well with salt and pepper, and baste well while cooking. Pigeon also benefits from an overnight marinade before cooking (see page 139 for marinade recipes). It can also be casseroled.

Pigeon with Figs

✦ SERVES 4 ✦

I met broadcaster Joan Whittle from Food on Friday *several years ago, when with* Life *magazine's wine and food editor Brian Hargreaves and Tony Tymon from British Airways we became the judging panel for* Life's *Food and Wine Awards. Joan gave me two of her favourite recipes: Pigeon with Figs and Quail with Mushrooms (page 36). Quail, partridge and small duck can be cooked with figs in the same way.*

2 tablespoons olive oil	425ml (15fl oz) chicken stock
4 oven-ready pigeons	3 tablespoons clear honey
1 medium onion, finely sliced	1 bouquet garni
1 large garlic clove, crushed	8 figs, fresh or tinned, cut in half
1 tablespoon brandy	salt and freshly ground black pepper

1 Heat the olive oil in a large pan. Brown the pigeons all over for 5 minutes and remove from the pan.

2 Add the onion and garlic to the pan and cook for a few minutes until softened. Stir in the brandy, stock, honey and bouquet garni. Return the pigeons to the pan, cover and simmer for 90 minutes. The pigeons are cooked when the juices run clear if you insert a sharp knife into the leg meat.

3 Remove the birds from the pan and keep them hot. Strain the cooking liquid into a small saucepan, and boil to reduce by half. Turn down the heat and carefully add the figs. Heat through for 3–4 minutes. Taste and season if necessary.

4 Cut the pigeons in half, remove the bones and arrange on a warmed serving dish, spooning over the sauce and the figs.

Grilled Breast of Pigeon with a Peach Salad and Hazelnut Dressing

✦ SERVES 4 ✦

This recipe comes from the Game Marketing Executive. I have added my own marinade.

8 pigeon breasts, skinned	25ml (1fl oz) olive oil
4 fresh peaches, halved and stoned	4 peppercorns
50g (2oz) roasted hazelnuts	pinch of salt
exotic salad leaves	juice and zest of 2 oranges
salt and freshly ground black pepper	

FOR THE MARINADE

100ml (4fl oz) port

100ml (4fl oz) red wine

1 teaspoon balsamic vinegar

50g (2oz) raisins

FOR THE VINAIGRETTE

2 tablespoons hazelnut oil

4 tablespoons extra virgin olive oil

2 tablespoons balsamic vinegar

1 tablespoon ground hazelnuts

1 Mix the marinade ingredients and marinate the pigeon breasts for 12 hours or overnight.

2 Heat the grill and cook the pigeon breasts for 5 minutes, basting with the marinade. Slice the cooked pigeon breasts lengthways.

3 Slice the peaches thinly and roughly chop the hazelnuts. Whisk the vinaigrette ingredients together in a bowl.

4 Toss the salad leaves in the vinaigrette and arrange on a large serving dish. Dip the pigeon slices in the vinaigrette and arrange on top of the leaves. Sprinkle with the chopped hazelnuts and peach slices and season with salt and pepper.

5 Serve with warm French bread and a glass of Chardonnay.

Pigeons in Pimlico

✦ **SERVES 6** ✦

This recipe originates in The Art of Cookery Made Plain and Easy, *by Hannah Glasse (1747): 'Take the livers, with some fat and lean ham or bacon, mushrooms, truffles, parsley, and sweet herbs; season with beaten mace, pepper and salt, beat all these together with two raw eggs, put it into the bellies, roll them all in a thin veal, over that a thin slice of bacon; wrap them up in white paper, spit them on a small spit, and roast them.'*
My version omits the truffle, but you can still see why the pigeons flew away from Pimlico.

6 oven-ready pigeons	4 slices of rindless streaky bacon, chopped
12 slices of rindless smoked bacon	50g (2oz) button mushrooms, sliced
50g (2oz) melted butter	1 tablespoon chopped parsley
Sauce Chasseur (page 144)	a pinch of mace
	1 teaspoon dried basil
FOR THE STUFFING	1 teaspoon anchovy essence
50g (2oz) white breadcrumbs	freshly ground black pepper
100g (4oz) cooked chicken livers, chopped	1 large egg, beaten with a little milk

1 Preheat the oven to 180°C/350°F/gas 4.

2 Mix together all the stuffing ingredients. Stuff the pigeons with the mixture and wrap 2 slices of bacon around each bird. Lightly brush 6 pieces of cooking foil with the butter and wrap each bird in foil. Place on a baking tray and bake in the centre of the preheated oven for 40 minutes.

3 Serve with Sauce Chasseur.

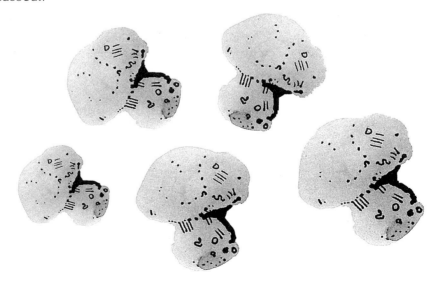

Pigeons in Red Wine

✦ Serves 4 ✦

This is a variation on the standard coq au vin recipe, low in calories and very healthy.

2 tablespoons olive oil	1 sprig of thyme
100g (4oz) rindless streaky bacon, chopped	4 tablespoons chopped parsley
600ml (1 pint) Game Stock (page 141)	1 bay leaf
225g (8oz) shallots	salt and freshly ground black pepper
225g (8oz) button mushrooms, trimmed	4 tablespoons brandy
1.75kg (4lb) boneless pigeon meat, skin removed	1 bottle of good Burgundy
3 tablespoons seasoned flour	15g (½oz) flour
2 garlic cloves, finely chopped	15g (½oz) butter, softened
	chopped parsley to garnish

1 Preheat the oven to 170°C/325°F/gas 3.

2 Heat the olive oil in a large flameproof casserole and sauté the pieces of bacon for 2 minutes. Add the shallots and mushrooms and cook for a further 3 minutes, then remove the bacon, shallots and mushrooms from the casserole to a warm plate.

3 Toss the pigeon meat in the seasoned flour, add to the casserole and sauté for 8 minutes, turning frequently. Add the bacon, shallots, mushrooms, garlic, thyme, parsley, bay leaf, salt and pepper and Game Stock. Cover the casserole and cook in the preheated oven for 35 minutes.

4 Remove the pigeon pieces, bacon and vegetables from the casserole and keep them warm. Skim off any excess fat from the juices. Warm the brandy pour into the casserole and ignite, allowing it to burn out for at least 2 minutes.

5 Pour over the wine. Make a *beurre manié* by mixing the flour into the softened butter, and stir this into the sauce. Cook until the sauce is reduced by half. Strain into a clean casserole and add the pigeon meat, bacon and vegetables. Let it simmer in the oven for a further 20 minutes.

6 Sprinkle with chopped parsley and serve.

GROUSE

The grouse is the first game to come into season on 12 August – the Glorious Twelfth. This is two weeks before the partridge and six weeks before the pheasant. It is a native of wild heather moorland, and can be found in parts of Scotland, Ireland, Wales and England – it was introduced successfully into Dartmoor and Exmoor. It lives on heather and berries, which gives it a unique flavour, stronger than that of other game birds.

I like to hang my grouse for two days only, depending on the weather – the cooler it is the better. Some people hang them for longer. Grouse are in prime condition from the beginning of the season to the middle of October. You can buy them from specialist butchers, and larger supermarkets during the season. Allow one grouse per person.

I think grouse is best plainly roasted and served with a salad, the way Queen Victoria's chef Francatelli cooked it for Her Majesty, but to be successfully roasted the bird must be young. Birds of uncertain age can be pot-roasted, or made into pies or pâtés.

Roast Grouse with Bacon and Sauce Chasseur, Garnished with Dripping Triangles

✦ SERVES 4 ✦

At some time in its history one in every five grand houses throughout Great Britain and Europe will have had this recipe served during the cold winter nights.

50g (2oz) butter	8 slices of rindless streaky bacon
juice of 1 lemon	2 tablespoons fresh or dried thyme
225g (8oz) redcurrants or cranberries	50g (2oz) beef dripping
salt and freshly ground black pepper	2 slices of bread, cut into triangles
4 oven-ready grouse	300ml (10fl oz) Sauce Chasseur (page 144)

1 Preheat the oven to 200°C/400°F/gas 6. Melt the butter in a saucepan and add the lemon juice. Stir in the redcurrants or cranberries, season, and cook for 1 minute. Allow to cool. Fill the cavities of each bird with the currants and juice, seasoning the birds all over with salt and pepper.

2 Wrap 2 slices of bacon over each breast and sprinkle with thyme. Wrap each bird in buttered foil and place them breast down in a roasting tin. Roast in the preheated oven for 15 minutes, then remove the foil and roast for a further 10 minutes.

3 Heat the dripping in a frying pan and fry the bread triangles on both sides until golden brown.

4 Arrange the bread triangles on a large serving dish and put the grouse on top. Serve with Sauce Chasseur.

Honey Roast Grouse with Chestnuts and Game Chips

✦ **SERVES 4** ✦

It is important to use young grouse for this recipe to ensure that the meat is as tender as possible.

4 young grouse	**1 teaspoon paprika**
50g (2oz) butter, softened	**salt and freshly ground black pepper**
4 tablespoons honey	**3 tablespoons poppy seeds**
2 tablespoons lemon juice	**450g (1lb) peeled chestnuts**
1 tablespoon brown sugar	**Game Chips (page 149)**

1 Preheat the oven to 230°C/450°F/gas 8.

2 Put the grouse into a large ovenproof dish. Put the butter, honey, lemon juice, sugar, paprika, salt and pepper into a large bowl and mix thoroughly. Using a pastry brush, paint the mixture on to the surface of the grouse and bake in the centre of the preheated oven for 15 minutes.

3 Turn the grouse over and spoon the mixture over the top. Sprinkle with the poppy seeds and return to the oven for a further 15 minutes.

4 Reduce the heat to 180°C/350°F/gas 4. Add the peeled chestnuts and return to the oven for 12 minutes.

5 Arrange the birds on a serving dish, pour over the juices and serve with the chestnuts and game chips.

Roast Capercailzie with Orange and Cranberry Stuffing

✦ **SERVES 4** ✦

The capercailzie is a type of grouse found in woodland areas, preferring pine woods and small bog patches with abundant berries.

100g (4oz) melted butter	**FOR THE STUFFING**
juice of 1 orange	50g (2oz) butter
6 tablespoons cranberry juice	4 tablespoons shallots, finely chopped
5 tablespoons sweet white wine	1 tablespoon freshly chopped mint
2 tablespoons freshly chopped mint	225g (8oz) Cumberland sausagemeat
2 capercailzie, dressed	juice and finely grated zest of 1 orange
300ml (10fl oz) Sauce Poivrade (page 000)	225g (8oz) fresh cranberries
10 small pork sausages	100g (4oz) fresh brown breadcrumbs
10 small slices of rindless streaky bacon	2 tablespoons finely chopped fresh parsley
3 oranges, sliced	salt and freshly ground black pepper
cranberry jelly	
2 sprigs of parsley	

1 Preheat the oven to 200°C/400°F/gas 6.

2 Put the melted butter into a bowl with the orange juice, cranberry juice, wine and mint.

3 To make the stuffing, fry the shallots in the butter for 4 minutes, then add the mint and cook for 1 minute. Put in a large bowl with all the other stuffing ingredients and mix well. Stuff the birds with the mixture and place them on a rack in a large roasting tin. Wrap the sausages in the bacon.

4 Cook the birds in the preheated oven for 15 minutes. Baste with the butter and juice mixture, then lower the heat to 180°C/350°F/gas 4 and cook for 90 minutes, continuing to baste every 15 minutes. Place the sausages wrapped in bacon around the birds for the last 25 minutes of the cooking time.

5 Serve with the sausages in bacon, game chips, and a rich gravy made from the juices in the roasting pan. Garnish with orange slices, cranberry jelly and parsley.

Roast Blackcock with Raspberry Sauce

✦ **SERVES 4** ✦

Blackcock is another type of grouse, more widespread than the capercailzie and preferring more open country. For a special touch, sprinkle a little walnut oil over the saffron rice before serving.

2 large blackcock	25g (1oz) red peppers, cut into very fine strips
50g (2oz) butter	
2 tablespoons olive oil	25g (1oz) shredded leeks
150ml (5fl oz) fine cognac	salt and freshly ground black pepper
25g (1oz) plain flour	450g (1lb) fresh raspberries
150ml (5fl oz) raspberry juice	1 tablespoon chopped fresh tarragon
25g (1oz) courgettes, cut into very fine strips	150ml (5fl oz) fromage frais

1 Preheat the oven to 200°C/400°F/gas 6. Put the birds in a roasting tin and roast in the centre of the preheated oven for 20 minutes. Reduce the oven temperature to 180°C/350°F/gas 4 and cook for a further 25 minutes.

2 Heat the butter and oil in a large frying pan, add the cognac and cook for 2 minutes. Sprinkle lightly with the flour and cook for a further minute. Reduce the heat and add the raspberry juice, courgettes, peppers and leeks. Season with salt and pepper and simmer for 10 minutes, until the sauce is reduced and thickens. Add half the raspberries, the tarragon and the fromage frais and cook for a further 2 minutes.

3 Slice the meat thinly and arrange in a fan shape around the centre of a large warm plate. Surround with saffron rice, garnish with fresh raspberries and tarragon leaves, and serve with the sauce.

GUINEA FOWL

The guinea fowl is a semi-domesticated bird which originates from West Africa. It is now readily available in supermarkets and tastes like a cross between corn-fed chicken and a pheasant. Any recipe for pheasant or quail will also suit guinea fowl.

Nick White at Ashwood Foods has been developing British guinea fowl for thirty years. This versatile and appetizing bird can be prepared and cooked in a wide variety of ways, from the quick and simple to the complex and sophisticated. It is one of the finest game birds for roasting, barbecuing or casseroling.

Roast Guinea Fowl

✦ SERVES 4 ✦

This is the simplest treatment for guinea fowl.

1 Preheat the oven to 190°C/375°F/gas 5.

2 Place small peeled onions in the body cavity of the bird, sprinkle with a little olive oil, and season with salt and freshly ground black pepper. Cook in the centre of the preheated oven for 45 minutes, then add a little butter, baste, and raise the heat to 200°C/400°F/gas 6 for a final 15 minutes.

A Tenor's Fried Guinea Fowl

✦ SERVES 4 ✦

I created this dish back in the Seventies for a famous Italian tenor, who fell in love with my cooking. It is equally good for pheasant or quail.

2 guinea fowl, cut into portions	**FOR THE MARINADE**
150ml (5fl oz) olive oil	**1 large bunch of parsley, finely chopped**
seasoned plain flour	**juice and zest of 1 lemon**
2 eggs, beaten and seasoned	**1 teaspoon crushed fennel seed**
4 sprigs of fresh basil	**1 teaspoon chopped fresh basil**
Game Chips (page 149) to serve	**4 tablespoons extra virgin olive oil**
	salt and freshly ground black pepper

1 Put the guinea fowl in a deep casserole and sprinkle with the marinade ingredients. Leave in a cool place to marinate for 4 hours, turning the guinea fowl every 30 minutes.

2 Heat the olive oil in a deep frying pan. Remove the guinea fowl from the marinade and coat each piece with seasoned flour and beaten egg. When the olive oil is hot, add the guinea fowl and fry over a medium heat for 15–20 minutes, until golden brown. Remove the guinea fowl with a slotted spoon and drain on kitchen paper.

3 Serve the crisp pieces of guinea fowl on a large dish, garnished with fresh basil. Serve game chips with the guinea fowl, and put finger bowls with a slice of lemon on the table.

Suprême of Guinea Fowl Nell Gwynn

✦ SERVES 4 ✦

*Oranges are not the only fruit you can use for my Nell Gwynn recipe –
try strawberries, or a mixture of your favourite fruit.*

25ml (1fl oz) vegetable oil	50g (2oz) red peppers, cut into fine strips
1 tablespoon olive oil	50g (2oz) leeks, finely shredded
4 guinea fowl suprêmes	salt and freshly ground black pepper
150ml (5fl oz) orange brandy	3 large oranges, cut into segments, the
15g (½oz) plain flour	zest cut into very fine strips
150ml (5fl oz) freshly squeezed	2 tablespoons chopped fresh tarragon
orange juice	150ml (5fl oz) fromage frais
50g (2oz) courgettes, cut into fine strips	

1 Heat the oils in a large frying pan. Add the guinea fowl suprêmes and cook slowly until they are a light golden brown colour.

2 Add the orange brandy and cook for a further 3 minutes, then sprinkle lightly with the flour and cook for a further 2 minutes. Reduce the heat and add the orange juice. Stir in the strips of courgette, peppers and leek and season with salt and pepper.

3 Simmer for 4 minutes until the sauce reduces and thickens. Add half the orange segments and zest with the tarragon and fromage frais and cook for a further 3 minutes.

4 Arrange the suprêmes on 4 warmed plates, and pour over a little orange sauce. Garnish with the remaining orange segments and fresh tarragon leaves, and sprinkle with the remaining orange zest.

5 Serve on a bed of noodles or wild rice.

Guinea Fowl and Pork with Tarragon and Cider Sauce

✦ **SERVES 4** ✦

A quick and simple casserole and great if you have a slow cooker – just throw it in and leave it!

4 guinea fowl, jointed	1 teaspoon tomato purée
225g (8oz) pork fillet, diced	salt and freshly ground black pepper
2 tablespoons chopped fresh tarragon	15g (½oz) butter, softened
1 large onion, sliced	15g (½oz) flour
2 Bramley apples, peeled, cored and diced	3 tablespoons port
300ml (10fl oz) dry cider	1 apple, sliced
2 tablespoons honey	1 sprig of fresh tarragon
1 tablespoon English mustard	Game Chips (page 149) to serve

1 Preheat the oven to 230°C/450°F/gas 8.

2 Remove any fat or gristle from the guinea fowl and pork fillet and place the pieces into a deep buttered casserole. Cook in the preheated oven for 20 minutes.

3 Put the tarragon, onion, apples, cider, honey, mustard, tomato, salt and pepper into a bowl and mix thoroughly. Pour the mixture over the guinea fowl. Lower the oven to 150°C/300°F/gas 2, cover the casserole, and cook in the centre of the oven for 90 minutes.

4 Remove the guinea fowl and pork to a warmed serving dish. Pour the juices into a saucepan and bring to the boil. Blend the butter and flour to make a *beurre manié* and add to the pan to thicken the sauce. Add the port and boil rapidly for 3 minutes. Pour the hot sauce over the meats and garnish with apple slices and fresh tarragon. Serve with game chips.

Stir-Fried Guinea Fowl

✦ SERVES 4 ✦

Ark Foods in Diss, Norfolk, sent me this recipe, which I have adapted slightly.
It is important to ensure that the sesame seed oil does not burn.

60ml (2fl oz) sesame oil	1 tablespoon grated fresh ginger
6 guinea fowl suprêmes, thinly sliced	1 teaspoon five-spice powder
1 garlic clove, crushed	salt and freshly ground black pepper
2 bunches of spring onions, chopped	
1 red pepper, finely sliced	FOR THE SAUCE
1 green pepper, finely sliced	1 tablespoon cornflour
1 yellow pepper, finely sliced	2 tablespoons soy sauce
85g (3oz) mangetout, sliced	1 tablespoon oyster sauce
85g (3oz) baby sweetcorn, sliced	1 tablespoon sherry
85g (3oz) leek, finely sliced	60ml (2fl oz) chicken stock

1 Mix all the sauce ingredients thoroughly and set aside until required.

2 Heat the sesame oil in a wok or large frying pan. When it is hot add the sliced guinea fowl and the garlic and stir-fry for 4 minutes. Add the spring onions, peppers, mangetout, sweetcorn and leek and stir-fry for 2 minutes, adding the ginger, five-spice, salt and pepper. Stir-fry for a further minute then add the sauce mixture. Stir-fry for 2 more minutes, and serve with Chinese noodles.

GOOSE

The domestic goose is the type seen on sale in the UK – the sale of wild geese is prohibited by law, and so they will only be available to those who shoot their own.

Size varies according to breed and sex: the female bird grows to only two-thirds the size of the male. The male bird when adult is known as a gander, but in culinary parlance male and female birds are each called a goose when adult and either a gosling or green goose up to six months old. Commercially raised geese are often free-range, and a mature bird will reach 3.6–5kg (8–12lb), serving 6–8 people. When choosing a goose, look for pale fatty skin and a plump breast, showing that the bird is young. Older birds will be tough.

Goose is usually roasted whole, and can also be braised or pot-roasted. Jointed, it can be stewed or braised like duck. Like duck, too, care should be taken to prevent the bird sitting in its fat – use a rack in the roasting tin so that the fat will drip into the tin and can be collected. Goose fat is a delicacy, as is the liver, notoriously fattened in France to produce *foie gras*.

Roast Goose with Mint, Onion and Apple Stuffing

✦ **SERVES 4** ✦

Most people think of roast goose as a dish reserved for the festive season. But for a Sunday dinner on a cold winter's day, it becomes a meal to remember.

1 × 4.5kg (10lb) goose, cleaned	1 large onion, chopped
3 tablespoons orange juice	the goose liver, finely chopped
salt and freshly ground black pepper	175g (6oz) Cumberland sausagemeat
1 bunch of watercress	225g (8oz) white breadcrumbs
1 apple, sliced	1 teaspoon dried mint
1 sprig of fresh mint	225g (8oz) apple, cored and chopped
	1 teaspoon finely chopped lemon peel, soaked in 1 tablespoon of cider
FOR THE STUFFING	
50g (2oz) butter	salt and freshly ground black pepper

1 Preheat the oven to 170°C/325°F/gas 3.

2 Prick the goose all over with a fork. Rub the orange juice into the breast and season well with salt and pepper, including the cavity.

3 Melt the butter in a frying pan and gently fry the onion and goose liver for 3 minutes. Allow to cool, then mix with the rest of the stuffing ingredients. Stuff the cavity of the goose with the mixture.

4 Truss the goose and place it on a rack in a roasting tin.

5 The goose must be roasted slowly for 3 hours. For the first 30 minutes roast breast side up, then turn the goose over on to its breast and cook for 1 hour. Pour the excess fat into a jug, turn the goose back to breast side up, and cook for the final 90 minutes. Test if the goose is cooked by inserting a metal meat skewer into the leg: if the juices run clear it is cooked; if they are still pink cook for a further 20 minutes or until they run clear. Allow the goose to cool slightly before carving.

6 Serve the goose on a bed of watercress, garnished with apple slices and mint leaves.

7 Serve with game chips (page 149) or roast potatoes, green beans and giblet gravy (page 148).

Roast Goose with Orange Brandy Sauce

✦ SERVES 10 ✦

Another festive recipe. For Makentie. Stuff the goose with your favourite stuffing and chopped apples.

1 large 5–6kg (12–14lb) Norfolk goose	25g (1oz) plain flour
50g (2oz) butter	150ml (5fl oz) Demi-glace Sauce
2 tablespoons olive oil	(page 143)
50g (2oz) courgettes, cut into very	150ml (5fl oz) fresh orange juice
fine strips	3 fresh oranges, cut into segments, the
50g (2oz) red peppers, cut into very	zest cut into very fine strips
fine strips	2 tablespoons chopped fresh tarragon
50g (2oz) shredded leeks	150ml (5fl oz) fromage frais
salt and freshly ground black pepper	fresh tarragon to garnish
150ml (5fl oz) orange brandy	Game Chips (page 149) to serve

1 Preheat the oven to 200°C/400°F/gas 6. Roast the goose in the centre of the preheated oven for 60 minutes. Baste with the goose fat, reduce the oven temperature to 180°C/350°F/gas 4, and cook for a further 2 hours.

2 Heat the butter and oil in a large frying pan and add the courgettes, peppers and leeks. Season with salt and pepper and cook for 4 minutes. Add the orange brandy and cook for 2 minutes, then sprinkle lightly with the flour and cook for 5 minutes more.

3 Reduce the heat and add the demi-glace sauce and orange juice and simmer for 15 minutes, until the sauce is thick and reduced by at least half. Add half the orange segments and rind, stir in the tarragon and fromage frais and cook for a further 2 minutes.

4 Slice the goose meat thinly and arrange in a fan shape around the centre of a large warm serving dish with a little of the sauce. Garnish with the remaining orange segments, zest and some fresh tarragon leaves, and serve with game chips.

Maryland Style Goose Breast

✦ SERVES 4 ✦

This is a marvellous recipe for summer or winter. I created it after tasting a famous American brand of fried chicken several years ago, and it is also very good made with very lean wild turkey breast.

175g (6oz) plain flour

salt and freshly ground black pepper

1 teaspoon Italian seasoning

1 teaspoon dried tarragon

1 teaspoon fresh or dried rosemary

1 teaspoon paprika

2 eggs, beaten

120ml (4fl oz) semi-skimmed milk

2.3kg (5lb) boneless goose breast, cut into serving pieces

seasoned flour

150ml (5fl oz) vegetable oil

2 bananas, peeled and quartered

1 apple, cored and cut into rings

340g (10oz) frozen or canned sweetcorn with diced peppers

To serve

fresh watercress

Game Chips (page 149)

horseradish sauce

1 Preheat the oven to 170°C/325°F/gas 3.

2 Put the flour, salt, pepper, Italian seasoning, herbs and paprika into a large bowl and mix well. Make a well in the centre and add the eggs. Slowly add the milk, whisking until very smooth.

3 Coat the goose pieces with seasoned flour. Heat the oil in a large frying pan. Dip the goose pieces into the batter and fry until lightly browned all over – about 3 minutes. Place the goose pieces on a non-stick baking tray and bake in the centre of the preheated oven for 35 minutes.

4 Dip the banana and apple rings into the batter and fry for 3 minutes. Keep warm.

5 Add the sweetcorn to the leftover batter and make the mixture into little flat patty cakes. Fry them for 4 minutes on either side. Keep warm with the apple and banana fritters.

6 Arrange the goose on a bed of fresh watercress with the sweetcorn, apple and banana fritters, and serve with game chips and horseradish sauce.

WILD TURKEY

Wild turkey is native to America and is seldom used today. Turkey is often only thought of in Britain at times of celebration such as Easter and Christmas, yet this very versatile meat is becoming more and more popular throughout Europe. The Americans slowly pot-roast wild turkey and use it a great deal in casseroles.

Wild Turkey with Caramelized Onion and Apple

✦ **SERVES 4** ✦

The caramelized onions and apples make a wonderful sauce.

225g (8oz) pork fat, diced	25g (1oz) plain flour
50g (2oz) butter	600ml (20fl oz) Game Stock (page 141) or chicken stock
3 apples, peeled, cored and diced	
16 small onions or shallots	bouquet garni
4 tablespoons caster sugar	salt and freshly ground black pepper
1 wild turkey, trussed	

1 Preheat the oven to 200°C/400°F/gas 6.

2 Add the pork fat to a pan of boiling salted water, simmer for 3 minutes, drain and dry.

3 Melt the butter in a large frying pan and add the pork, apple and onions. Brown lightly for 3 minutes, then add the sugar and cook for about 5 minutes until caramelized. Remove the pork, apple and onions from the pan and keep warm.

4 Add the wild turkey to the pan and brown on all sides. Remove the turkey to a large roasting tin. Add the flour to the pan, cook until it begins to brown, then slowly blend in the stock. Pour the sauce over the turkey, add the bouquet garni, and cook in the preheated oven for 20 minutes per 450g (1lb). Remove the bouquet garni 10 minutes before the end of the cooking time.

5 Put the turkey on a large serving platter, surrounded by the pork, apple and caramelized onions. Serve the sauce separately.

Breast of Wild Turkey with a White Wine and Black Cherry Sauce

✦ SERVES 4 ✦

In this recipe the turkey is stuffed with a spinach mixture and served with a cherry sauce.

3 shallots, finely chopped	**FOR THE SAUCE**
75g (3oz) butter	25g (1oz) butter
100g (4oz) button mushrooms, thinly sliced	75g (3oz) fresh black cherries, stoned
75g (3oz) cooked spinach	2 shallots, chopped
salt and freshly ground black pepper	50g (2oz) button mushrooms, sliced
1 tablespoon fresh chervil	150ml (¼ pint) white wine
2 tablespoons Cointreau	150ml (¼ pint) chicken stock
4 wild turkey breasts	150ml (¼ pint) fromage frais
black cherries to garnish	1 tablespoon cherry brandy
	salt and freshly ground black pepper

1 Preheat the oven to 200°C/400°F/gas 6.

2 Sauté the shallots in 50g (2oz) of the butter until soft, then add the mushrooms and cook for 2 minutes more. Add the spinach, season, and cook for a further minute. Finally add the chervil and Cointreau. Stir well and allow to cool.

3 Slice each turkey breast lengthways to make a pocket and fill the pocket with the spinach mixture. Spread with the remaining butter, wrap in foil, and cook in the preheated oven for 35 minutes.

4 Meanwhile make the sauce. Melt the butter in a frying pan and sauté the cherries, shallots and mushrooms for 3 minutes. Add the white wine and chicken stock and boil to reduce the sauce to a quarter of the original amount. Add the fromage frais, cherry brandy and seasoning and reduce by half again.

5 Remove the wild turkey breasts from the foil, slice them thinly into a fan shape, and serve with the sauce, garnished with fresh black cherries.

Breast of Wild Turkey with Sun-Blush Tomatoes

✦ SERVES 4 ✦

Sun-blush tomatoes are readily available now in supermarkets.

4 wild turkey breast fillets	4 tablespoons sun-blush tomatoes
salt and freshly ground black pepper	1 tablespoon honey
25g (1oz) butter	100g (4oz) fresh or frozen raspberries
50g (2oz) carrots, finely chopped	25g (1oz) flour
50g (2oz) shallots, finely chopped	1 tablespoon Worcestershire sauce
1 tablespoon lemon juice	sun-dried tomatoes, raspberries and lemon
150ml (5fl oz) Game Stock (page 141)	slices to garnish
or chicken stock	

1 Trim and score the turkey breasts and season them well all over. Melt the butter in a frying pan and cook the turkey breasts for about 3 minutes on each side.

2 Add the carrots, shallots, the lemon juice and a little of the stock. Add the sun-blush tomatoes, simmer for 4 minutes, then add the honey and raspberries and sprinkle with the flour. Allow to cook for 3 minutes, seasoning with freshly ground black pepper. Add the Worcestershire sauce.

3 Remove the turkey fillets from the pan, allowing the sauce to continue simmering. Slice the breasts lengthways into 4mm (¼ inch) pieces. Pour a little of the sauce on to a serving dish, arrange the turkey fillets in a fan shape, and garnish with sun-dried tomatoes, fresh raspberries and lemon slices.

Traditional Christmas Jugged Turkey

✦ SERVES 6 ✦

A recipe that makes use of older grouse as well as turkey meat.

50g (2oz) butter	1 teaspoon cinnamon
75g (3oz) rindless streaky bacon, chopped	2 cloves, crushed
675g (1½lb) turkey meat, diced	zest of ½ lemon
350g (12oz) grouse meat, diced	salt and freshly ground black pepper
1 onion, roughly chopped	600ml (20fl oz) chicken stock
2 carrots, diced	4 tablespoons brandy
2 sticks celery, chopped	25g (1oz) plain flour
4 tablespoons fresh cranberries	5 tablespoons port

1 Put the butter and bacon into a large saucepan and cook for 3 minutes. Add the turkey and grouse, cook for 7 minutes until browned, then add the vegetables, cranberries, spices and lemon zest. Season well.

2 Pour over the stock and brandy and bring to the boil. Cover the pan, put a weight or something else heavy on to the lid, and simmer for 90 minutes on a low heat.

3 Mix the flour with a little port to make a paste and add to the pan. Cook for 5 minutes more, then add the remaining port.

4 Serve with crusty bread and a bottle of dry red wine.

Turkey Bourguignon

✦ SERVES 4 ✦

A variation on the coq-au-vin theme.

100g (4oz) rindless streaky bacon	1 teaspoon chopped fresh parsley
50g (2oz) butter	650g (1½lb) wild turkey meat, diced
24 shallots	salt and freshly ground black pepper
225g (8oz) small button mushrooms	150ml (5fl oz) Burgundy
2 garlic cloves, crushed	450ml (15fl oz) chicken stock
1 teaspoon dried thyme	1 tablespoon cornflour

1 Preheat the oven to 180°C/350°F/gas 4.

2 Cut each bacon rasher into 5 or 6 pieces. Heat the butter in a large frying pan and add the bacon, shallots, mushrooms, garlic, thyme and parsley. Cook gently for 10 minutes, then add the turkey meat and cook for a further 5 minutes. Pour the mixture into a deep casserole, season, and add the wine and stock and cook in the preheated oven for 2 hours.

3 Thicken the red wine sauce with the cornflour, blended with a little water, and serve.

Sticky Breast of Turkey

✦ SERVES **4** ✦

A *truly sticky, mouthwatering coating for the turkey breasts.*

salt and freshly ground black pepper	225g (8oz) shallots, sliced
2 boneless wild turkey breasts	100ml (4fl oz) port
25ml (1fl oz) olive oil	25ml (1fl oz) brandy
25g (1oz) unsalted butter	1 tablespoon red wine vinegar
75g (3oz) honey	1 teaspoon pink peppercorns
75g (3oz) blackcurrants	orange slices and mint leaves to garnish

1 Preheat the oven to 230°C/450°F/gas 8.

2 Season the turkey breasts and score with a sharp knife. Heat the oil and butter in a roasting tin and seal the turkey breasts over a high heat until lightly browned.

3 Put all the other ingredients into a bowl and mix thoroughly. Coat the breasts thickly with the honey mixture and cook in the preheated oven for 35 minutes, basting every 5 minutes with the mixture.

4 Slice each breast into slices lengthways and keep warm in a low oven.

5 Put the honey marinade from the turkey and any mixture that is left into a saucepan and reduce over a high heat until it thickens. Pour the sauce over the slices of turkey and put under a hot grill for about 2 minutes before serving.

6 Garnish with slices of orange and mint leaves.

FIRST CATCH YOUR HARE

Rabbit and hare have been used in the cookery of our islands for centuries. The well-known saying 'First catch your hare' is attributed to Hannah Glasse (1708–70) in her book The Art of Cookery Made Plain and Easy, published in 1747. Rabbit is available both farmed and wild, and is available all year round at butchers and supermarkets, while hare must not be sold from March to July.

Both rabbit and hare can be bought skinned and trimmed, and are a very healthy food – fat-free and very low in cholesterol.

SKINNING A HARE OR RABBIT

Your butcher will do this for you, or you can do it yourself. First gut the hare or rabbit and remove the innards. Sever each leg at the first joint. Cut through the skin around the hind legs, just below the tail, peeling the skin down. Tie the hind legs together, place on a firm hook, and pull the skin down over the body to the end of the forelegs. Remove the head and wash the hare or rabbit with cold water. Rub salt into the cavity and over the complete carcass, and leave for an hour. Wash again thoroughly, then cut the hare or rabbit into joints.

It is now ready for use.

RABBIT

The meat of farmed rabbit is light and delicate, very like chicken, and is ideal in those recipes where chicken could also be used, such as sautés, curries and casseroles. Wild rabbits have a gamy flavour and can be hung for up to a week, though young wild rabbits should be skinned and cooked within 2 days, and must not be hung.

Both farmed and wild rabbit are ideal for making pies and pâtés.

Roasted Rabbit

✦ SERVES **4** ✦

Young rabbit is best for roasting.

FOR THE MARINADE	
425ml (15fl oz) red wine	50ml (2fl oz) olive oil
1 large onion, sliced	1 sprig of rosemary
3 garlic cloves	6 juniper berries
2 tablespoons lemon juice	salt and freshly ground black pepper
	2 young rabbits

1 Mix all the marinade ingredients together in a deep bowl. Add the rabbit, cover with the marinade, and chill for 12 hours or overnight. Preheat the oven to 200°C/400°F/gas 6. Put the rabbit with its marinade into a roasting tin and cook in the preheated oven for 40–60 minutes, basting with the marinade every 15 minutes.

Rabbit Cooked in Port with a Rum and Raisin Sauce

✦ SERVES **4–6** ✦

A combination of foods used on the Tall Ships, when they came to Liverpool, gave me the idea for this recipe. It is a dish that might have been served on Nelson's flagship Victory.

2 rabbits, boned	150g (5oz) raisins
50g (2oz) butter	150ml (5fl oz) Demi-glace Sauce (page 143)
juice and zest of 1 lemon	salt and freshly ground black pepper
6 tablespoons port	4 tablespoons dark rum
1 tablespoon white wine	150ml (1/4 pint) sour cream

1 Cut the rabbit meat into thin slices. Heat the butter in a frying pan, add the rabbit, and cook gently for 10 minutes, turning frequently until the meat is lightly coloured. Add the lemon juice and zest and the port and cook for a further 5 minutes.

2 Remove the rabbit from the pan, arrange in a serving dish. Keep warm in a low oven.

3 Return the pan with the rabbit juices to the heat. Add the wine and raisins and simmer for 5 minutes. Add the demi-glace and simmer until the sauce is reduced by half. Season with salt and pepper, add the dark rum, and cook for a further 5 minutes. Finally add the cream and simmer until reduced by half again.

4 Remove the rabbit from the oven, pour the sauce into the centre of the dish and serve immediately.

Rabbit with Rosemary Cider Sauce

✦ SERVES 4 ✦

Quick and simple and great if you have a slow cooker – just throw it all in and leave it!
The strength of the rosemary complements the rabbit.

8 slices of rindless streaky bacon	1 tablespoon English mustard
8 rabbit portions, about 175g (6oz) each	1 teaspoon tomato purée
1 tablespoon fresh rosemary leaves	salt and freshly ground black pepper
1 large onion, sliced	15g (½oz) butter, softened
300ml (10fl oz) dry cider	15g (½oz) flour
150ml (5fl oz) Sauce Poivrade (page 145)	1 apple, sliced
2 tablespoons honey	1 sprig of fresh rosemary

1 Preheat the oven to 230°C/450°F/gas 8.

2 Wrap a slice of bacon around each piece of rabbit and secure with a wooden cocktail stick. Put the rabbit into a deep buttered casserole and cook in the preheated oven for 20 minutes. Remove the cocktail sticks and return the rabbit to the casserole.

3 Put the rosemary, onion, cider, Sauce Poivrade, honey, mustard, tomato purée, salt and pepper into a bowl and mix thoroughly. Pour this mixture over the rabbit. Cover the casserole, lower the heat to 150°C/300°F/gas 2, and cook in the centre of the oven for 90 minutes.

4 Remove the rabbit and bacon to a warm serving dish. Pour the liquid from the casserole into a saucepan and heat, thickening the sauce with a *beurre manié* made by blending the softened butter with the flour. Pour the hot sauce over the rabbit and garnish with slices of apple and rosemary leaves.

Braised Rabbit with Black Pudding and Cider Sauce

✦ SERVES 4 ✦

If you don't like black pudding you can try this recipe using prunes instead.
You will then have the French dish known as lapin aux pruneaux.

900g (2lb) boneless rabbit meat, diced	150ml (5fl oz) Game Stock (page 141)
50g (2oz) seasoned flour	or chicken stock
25g (1oz) cooking oil	150ml (5fl oz) cider
450g (1lb) baby onions or shallots, sliced	1 teaspoon Worcestershire sauce
225g (8oz) black pudding, thinly sliced	salt and freshly ground black pepper

1 Preheat the oven to 150°C/300°F/gas 2.

2 Coat the meat in the seasoned flour. Heat the oil in a large frying pan and brown the meat all over. Remove the meat to a large deep casserole and sprinkle with the sliced onions.

3 Add the black pudding to the frying pan and fry slowly on both sides. Add the stock and cider and simmer for 15 minutes. Add the Worcestershire sauce, taste, then season with salt and pepper.

4 Pour the sauce and black pudding over the meat in the casserole. Cover with a lid or cooking foil. Place in the centre of the preheated oven and cook for 90 minutes, until the meat is very tender.

5 Serve with creamed potatoes.

Rabbit Cacciatore with Basil and Sun-Blush Tomatoes

✦ SERVES 4 ✦

A wonderful summertime recipe that I created for Louisa Ayland of the Game Marketing Executive.

1 boneless rabbit	**2 garlic cloves, crushed**
25g (1oz) seasoned flour	**285g (10oz) chopped tomatoes**
4 tablespoons olive oil	**1 tablespoon tomato purée**
25g (1oz) butter	**1 teaspoon honey**
150ml (5fl oz) chicken stock	**2 sprigs of fresh basil**
150ml (5fl oz) white wine	**4 tablespoons fromage frais**
1 onion, sliced	**350g (12oz) fresh or dried tagliatelle**
1 green pepper, sliced	**2 tablespoons chopped fresh basil**
50g (2oz) sun-blush tomatoes	**2 tablespoons sun-dried tomatoes, sliced**

1 Coat the rabbit portions in the seasoned flour. Heat the oil and butter in a large saucepan or flameproof casserole and brown the rabbit pieces all over. Add the stock and wine and cook for a further 20 minutes, until the liquid is reduced by half.

2 Sprinkle with the onion, pepper, sun-blush tomatoes, garlic, chopped tomatoes, tomato purée, honey and sprigs of basil. Give everything a good stir and simmer gently for a further 15 minutes.

3 Remove the rabbit and the basil sprigs to a warm serving dish and boil the sauce to reduce again by half. Stir in the fromage frais and keep the sauce just warm.

4 Meanwhile cook the tagliatelle in boiling salted water according to the packet instructions, and drain.

5 Put the tagliatelle on a large warm serving dish, topped with the rabbit pieces and sauce. Sprinkle with the chopped basil and sliced sun-dried tomatoes.

Rabbit Curry

✦ **SERVES 6** ✦

*Rabbit and curry go together perfectly. Furred game is ideal for curries — in this recipe you can
also use hare, wild boar or venison. Never overcook the game when making a
curry, and if possible make it 24 hours before you actually eat it.*

900g (2lb) boneless rabbit, diced	1 teaspoon chilli powder
50g (2oz) flour, seasoned with	1 teaspoon ground cardamom
1 teaspoon paprika, salt and freshly	1 teaspoon crushed cloves
ground black pepper	1 teaspoon ground cinnamon
2 tablespoons olive oil	1 teaspoon ground cumin
25g (1oz) butter	1 teaspoon ground coriander
1 onion, sliced	2 tablespoons tomato purée
450g (1lb) shallots	300ml (10fl oz) chicken stock
1 red pepper, chopped	150ml (5fl oz) red wine
1 green pepper, chopped	1 × 420g (14oz) tin of chopped tomatoes
1 teaspoon paprika	150ml (5fl oz) sour cream
1 teaspoon Tabasco	1 sprig of parsley
1 teaspoon grated fresh ginger	

1 Toss the rabbit generously in the seasoned flour. Heat the olive oil and butter in a
flameproof casserole and fry the onion, shallots and peppers for 3 minutes. Add the rabbit and
cook for a further 10 minutes. Sprinkle with the paprika, Tabasco, ginger, chilli powder,
cardamom, cloves, cinnamon, cumin and coriander and leave for 4 hours.

2 Preheat the oven to 170°C/325°F/gas 3.

3 Add the tomato purée, stock, wine and chopped tomatoes to the casserole, cover, and cook
in the centre of the preheated oven for 3 hours.

4 Remove from the oven and leave to cool. Refrigerate for 24 hours. Reheat, add the sour
cream, and garnish with the parsley.

Rabbit Jambalaya

✦ **SERVES 4** ✦

Prime Minister Tony Blair loves rabbit, and recently enjoyed this spicy rice dish during a visit from President Bill Clinton.

1.35kg (3lb) rabbit meat

50ml (2fl oz) olive oil

2 large onions, chopped

1 celery stick, chopped

1 green pepper, diced

225g (8oz) button mushrooms, sliced

225g (8oz) York ham, diced

1 × 400g (14oz) tin of chopped tomatoes

150ml (5fl oz) tomato juice

1 teaspoon Tabasco

225g (8oz) uncooked long-grain rice

425ml (15fl oz) Game Stock (page 141) or chicken stock

FOR THE SEASONING

2 bay leaves

1 teaspoon sea salt

1 teaspoon freshly ground black pepper

2 garlic cloves, crushed

1 teaspoon cayenne pepper

1 teaspoon freshly chopped red chillies

1 Cut the rabbit meat into 1cm (½ inch) dice.

2 Blend all the seasoning ingredients together and reserve.

3 Heat the oil in a large deep frying pan, add all the vegetables and stir-fry for 5 minutes. Add the rabbit, ham, tomatoes, tomato juice and Tabasco, and stir in the seasoning mixture. Simmer for 15 minutes.

4 Add the rice and stock and cook for about 15 minutes, stirring every 5 minutes, until the rice is firm, slightly moist but not too dry and the stock is completely absorbed.

5 Serve on a large serving dish, accompanied by garlic bread and a rich claret.

Rigatoni with Rabbit and Cream Sauce

✦ SERVES 4 ✦

Game goes well with pasta. The larger pasta shapes such as rigatoni
and fusilli complement this type of sauce best.

75g (3oz) butter	150ml (5fl oz) double cream
450g (1lb) rabbit meat, trimmed and thinly sliced	2 tablespoons olive oil
	450g (1lb) dried rigatoni
175g (6oz) button mushrooms, sliced	2 sprigs of fresh basil
1 teaspoon mustard	100g (4oz) butter
a pinch of minced fresh ginger	4 slices of hot toast, cut into triangles,
salt and freshly ground black pepper	to serve
2 tablespoons dry sherry	sprigs of fresh parsley

1 Preheat the oven to 190°C/375°F/gas 5.

2 Melt 75g (3oz) butter in a large saucepan and gently fry the rabbit for 15 minutes. Remove the rabbit from the pan with a slotted spoon, put in an ovenproof dish and keep warm. Add the mushrooms to the frying pan. Add the mustard, ginger, salt and pepper, cook for 2 minutes, then add the sherry and cream. Cook for a further 3 minutes, then pour the sauce over the rabbit. Bake in the preheated oven for 20 minutes.

3 Meanwhile bring a large pan of salted water to the boil. Add the olive oil, rigatoni and 1 sprig of basil and boil rapidly for 10 minutes or until the pasta is *al dente*. Drain and place in a serving dish with 100g (4oz) butter and the second sprig of basil. Serve the rabbit sauce separately, garnished with triangles of warm toast and sprigs of fresh parsley.

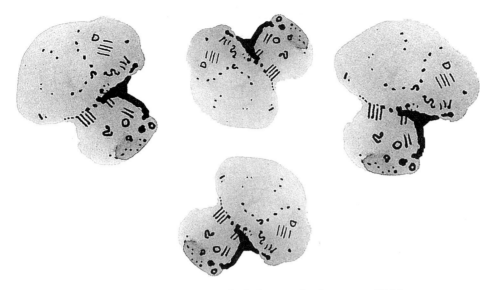

Rabbit with Fusilli

✦ **SERVES 6–8** ✦

A good rustic dish served with red wine and crusty bread.

50ml (2fl oz) olive oil	450g (1lb) dried fusilli
2 large onions, chopped	
1 celery stick, chopped	**FOR THE SEASONING**
1 green pepper, diced	2 bay leaves
225g (8oz) button mushrooms, sliced	1 teaspoon sea salt
1.35kg (3lb) rabbit meat, diced	1 teaspoon freshly ground black pepper
225g (8oz) York ham, diced	2 garlic cloves, crushed
1 × 420g (14oz) tin of chopped tomatoes	1 teaspoon cayenne pepper
150ml (5fl oz) tomato juice	1 teaspoon chopped fresh red chilli
1 teaspoon Tabasco	
425ml (15fl oz) Game Stock (page 141) or chicken stock	

1 Blend all the seasoning ingredients together and set aside.

2 Heat the oil in a large deep frying pan, add all the vegetables, and stir-fry for 5 minutes. Add the rabbit, ham, tomatoes, tomato juice, Tabasco and the seasoning mixture. Simmer for 15 minutes.

3 Bring the stock to the boil, add the fusilli, and cook for 10 minutes or until *al dente*. Drain the pasta, place on a large warm serving dish, top with the rabbit sauce and serve with chunks of bread.

HARE

There are two types of hare: the English hare, commonly known as the brown hare, and the blue hare which is native to Scotland. Like rabbit, hare is ideal for casseroles. Young hares are very good roasted.

A fully grown hare will provide meat for 6–8 people. A leveret should give enough for 4–6.

A leveret or young hare will have small white teeth, while the oldie's teeth will be large and yellow. Hare should be hung head downwards, ungutted, for a week. Older hare will benefit from a marinade (see page 139), but young ones can simply be basted with a little butter while cooking.

Hare Casserole

✦ SERVES 4 ✦

The forests of Europe have always been abundant in hare, and in the early sixteenth century their pelts were used for clothing. This was a favourite recipe at that time, and is still quite popular today. It can be made with either hare or rabbit.

100g (4oz) rindless streaky bacon	1 teaspoon chopped fresh thyme
900g (2lb) boneless hare or	1 teaspoon chopped fresh parsley
rabbit meat, chopped	salt and freshly ground black pepper
4 potatoes, chopped	600ml (20fl oz) Game Stock (page 141)
3 onions, sliced	150ml (5fl oz) Espagnole Sauce (page 143)
2 carrots, sliced	15g (½oz) butter, softened
100g (4oz) mushrooms, quartered	15g (½oz) flour

1 Preheat the oven to 170°C/325°F/gas 3.

2 Cut each bacon rasher into 5 or 6 pieces.

3 Layer the rabbit or hare, bacon and vegetables in a casserole and sprinkle with the herbs, seasoning well with salt and pepper. Pour over the stock and Espagnole sauce and cook in the preheated oven for 2 hours. Shortly before serving, thicken the sauce with a *beurre manié* made by blending the softened butter with the flour.

4 Serve with red cabbage and thick crusty bread.

Jugged Hare with Potato Herb Dumplings

✦ **SERVES 4** ✦

Jugging is one of the oldest methods of cookery. Game or other meat would be placed into a jug with a marinade, the jug covered and placed in a pot half filled with water, which was then boiled for several hours.

50g (2oz) butter

75g (3oz) rindless streaky bacon, chopped

675g (1½lb) boneless hare meat or

1 large hare, jointed

1 onion, roughly chopped

2 carrots, diced

2 celery sticks, chopped

zest of ½ lemon

salt and freshly ground black pepper

600ml (20fl oz) chicken stock

150ml (5fl oz) port

25g (1oz) plain flour

FOR THE POTATO HERB DUMPLINGS

350g (12oz) mashed potato

1 egg, beaten

salt and freshly ground black pepper

a generous pinch of mixed herbs

50g (2oz) seasoned flour

25g (1oz) semolina

2 tablespoons milk

1 Place all the ingredients for the dumplings into a bowl and mix thoroughly. Shape into small balls and place to one side until required.

2 Put the butter and bacon into a large saucepan and cook for 3 minutes. Add the hare, cook for 7 minutes until the hare is browned, then add the vegetables and lemon zest. Season well.

3 Pour over the stock and half the port and bring to the boil. Cover the pan, place a weight or something heavy on to the pan lid, and simmer for 3 hours on a low heat.

4 Mix the flour to a paste with a little port, and add to the hare. Cook for 3 minutes, then add the rest of the port. Add the dumplings, cover the pan, and simmer for a further 20 minutes.

5 Serve with crusty bread and dry red wine.

Hare in a Mushroom and Burgundy Sauce

✦ SERVES 8 ✦

This dish can be ruined by over-cooking and by using cheap wine. Always use a good-quality Burgundy for hare and rabbit recipes.

2.3kg (5lb) hare, jointed into 8 pieces	1 sprig of thyme
2 tablespoons olive oil	4 tablespoons finely chopped parsley
100g (4oz) rindless streaky bacon, cut into pieces	1 bay leaf
	salt and freshly ground black pepper
600ml (1 pint) chicken stock	4 tablespoons brandy
225g (8oz) shallots	1 bottle of Burgundy
225g (8oz) button mushrooms, trimmed	2 tablespoons cornflour
3 tablespoons seasoned flour	Game Chips (page 149) to serve
2 garlic cloves, finely chopped	

1 Preheat the oven to 170°C/325°F/gas 3. Make sure all the excess fat and skin is removed from the hare.

2 In a large flameproof casserole, heat the olive oil. Sauté the bacon for 2 minutes, then add the shallots and mushrooms. Cook for a further 3 minutes, then remove the bacon, mushrooms and shallots from the casserole to a warm plate.

3 Toss the pieces of hare in the seasoned flour and sauté for 10 minutes, turning the hare every 3 minutes. Add the bacon, shallots, mushrooms, stock, garlic, thyme, half the parsley and the bay leaf. Season with salt and pepper. Cover the casserole and cook in the preheated oven for 60 minutes.

4 Remove the hare pieces, bacon and vegetables from the casserole and keep them warm. Skim off any excess fat from the hare juices. Warm the brandy, pour it into the casserole and ignite, allowing it to burn for at least 2 minutes. Pour over the Burgundy, reserving at least a glassful. Cook until the wine is reduced by half its original quantity.

5 Add a little wine from the reserved glass to the cornflour and stir to a paste. Add to the sauce, whisking it in. Let the sauce cook for 4 minutes, then strain into a clean casserole. Add the hare, bacon and vegetables and return the casserole to the oven for a further 45 minutes.

6 Garnish with the remaining chopped parsley and serve with game chips.

Creamy Hare and Wild Mushroom Curry

✦ **Serves 6–8** ✦

*If you don't like wild mushrooms use button or oyster mushrooms, and for
extra flavour use a hot curry paste instead of mild.*

25g (1oz) vegetable oil	2 tablespoons Worcestershire sauce
900g (2lb) boneless hare meat, diced	2 tablespoons creamed coconut
50g (2oz) seasoned flour	pinch of ginger
450g (1lb) wild mushrooms, roughly chopped	2 tablespoons mild curry paste
300ml (10fl oz) chicken stock	salt and freshly ground black pepper
	150ml (5fl oz) double cream

1 Preheat the oven to 150°C/300°F/gas 2.

2 Heat the oil in a large frying pan. Toss the hare in the seasoned flour and brown it all over. Put the hare in a large deep casserole.

3 Add the mushrooms to the pan and fry slowly in the hare juices. Add the stock, Worcestershire sauce, coconut, ginger and curry paste, and season with salt and pepper.

4 Pour the sauce over the hare and cover the casserole with a lid or cooking foil. Place in the centre of the preheated oven and cook for 2 hours, until the hare is very tender. Stir in the cream, cook for a further 10 minutes, and serve with wild rice.

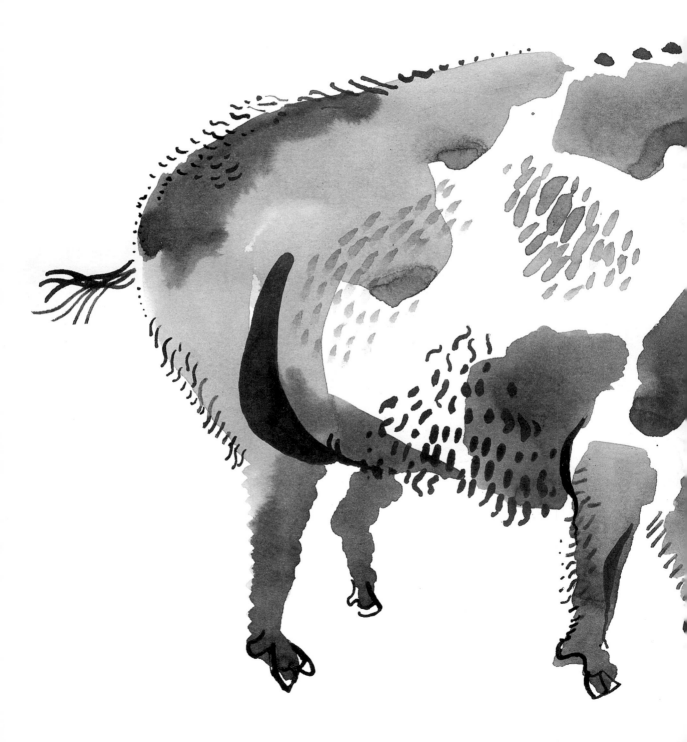

THE THRILL OF THE CHASE

Since time immemorial man has hunted for food. Hunting was a necessity for man's existence. Centuries of living in this way made hunting very deeply rooted in the human experience, and when it was no longer necessary as a means of livelihood, it remained as an almost universal sport.

Hunting was a sport among the ancient Egyptians, the Greeks and the Romans, and the English and French, led by their kings, became particularly fond of it. Edward the Confessor adored hunting, as did William the Conqueror. Monarchs such as Henry VIII and Elizabeth I of England and Henri IV of France enjoyed hunting as one of their major recreational activities.

Hunting is still a prime sport in Britain, and this chapter concentrates on the larger species of game: venison and wild boar.

VENISON

Venison, commonly known as 'the noble flesh', has almost always been associated with kings, queens and the rich and favoured of the world. The word 'venison' comes from the Latin *venari*, to hunt, and was formerly applied not only to the flesh of deer but to all animals killed in the chase and used for food, such as the wild boar and the hare.

Nowadays we can eat venison all year round, because it is farmed and available in our butchers and supermarkets as well as by mail order (see Useful Addresses, page 155). Wild venison is seasonal. Bucks come into season in May and remain the prime choice until September, when the does are in season at least until the New Year. If in doubt, ask your butcher for advice.

Venison is a red meat with a wonderful flavour, similar to beef but richer and gamier. The flavour varies according to how long it has been hung. It is a very healthy meat to eat, being low in fat, low in calories and high in protein. The meat is at its best in mature animals of 18–24 months.

The meat of the buck is better than that of the doe. The red deer and the fallow deer are the best species in Britain. The deer is divided into the hindquarters and forequarters. From the hindquarters the cuts of leg or loin together form the haunch, which is one of the most popular cuts (along with the saddle). The best cuts from the forequarters are the neck and best end of neck, breast and shoulder.

Immediately after killing, all venison must be hung in a cool and airy place away from flies for 2–3 weeks. When choosing venison, it is important to look at it carefully: the fat must be thick, bright and clear and the hoof cleft very smooth, close and clean. If the venison has been hung properly, the vein in the neck will remain bluish in colour, not yellow or green.

Venison is ideally suited to roasting and casseroling, and the more tender cuts can be grilled or stir-fried. Choose the haunch or saddle for roasting, or the cheaper boned rolled shoulder.

Traditional Roast Venison

✦ Serves 6 ✦

The best venison cuts for roasting are the haunch and saddle.

2.3kg (5lb) haunch of venison	1 large onion, sliced
175g (6oz) butter	1 leek, sliced
8 cloves	2 sprigs of fresh thyme
juice and grated rind of 1 orange	1 bay leaf
25g (1oz) seasoned flour	6 juniper berries
6 sprigs of fresh rosemary	1 teaspoon grated fresh ginger
Rowan Jelly (page 146)	1 teaspoon black peppercorns
	3 tablespoons balsamic vinegar
FOR THE MARINADE	3 tablespoons olive oil
300ml (10fl oz) red wine	2 garlic cloves, chopped
1 carrot, sliced	1 tablespoon soft brown sugar

1 Place all the marinade ingredients into a large saucepan and bring to the boil. Simmer for 15 minutes, then allow to cool.

2 Place the venison haunch into a large deep serving dish. Pour over the marinade, cover and place in a cool place for 24 hours, turning the meat every 6 hours.

3 Remove the venison from the marinade. Spread with the butter, sprinkle with the orange rind and juice and stick the cloves into the meat. Place in a deep roasting tin. Preheat the oven to 180°C/350°F/gas 4 and roast for 25 minutes per 450g (1lb), basting every 30 minutes – about 2 hours for a 2.3kg (5lb) haunch.

4 Remove the venison from the roasting tin to a large serving dish, and keep warm in the oven while you make the sauce.

5 Pour the juices from the roasting tin into a saucepan, add the flour, and cook for 2 minutes. Slowly add the marinade, bring to the boil, and simmer until it is reduced by half. Strain the sauce through a fine sieve into a sauceboat. Garnish the venison with sprigs of fresh rosemary, and serve with the sauce and with rowan jelly.

Roast Loin of Venison

✦ **SERVES 4–6** ✦

Cold roast venison is delicious served with rowan jelly.

2.8kg (6lb) loin of venison	2 tablespoons redcurrant jelly, plus more to serve
salt and freshly ground black pepper	
2 sprigs of fresh thyme	Game Chips (page 149), to serve
3 tablespoons juniper berries	

1 Preheat the oven to 180°C/350°F/gas 4. Put the venison into a roasting tin, season with salt and pepper and add the thyme and juniper berries.

2 Roast for 40 minutes per 450g/1lb, basting every 20 minutes. Allow the meat to cool for 10 minutes. Then coat with redcurrant jelly and cook for a further 20 minutes.

3 Slice the venison and arrange in a circle on a serving dish with generous dollops of redcurrant jelly. Serve hot or cold with game chips.

Venison Spare Ribs with Garlic Sauce

✦ SERVES 8 ✦

The garlicky sauce is delicious with these spare ribs.

2kg (4lb) venison ribs, cut into 7.5cm
(3 inch) lengths

1 tablespoon cornflour mixed with
2 tablespoons dry sherry

5 tablespoons sour cream or yoghurt

FOR THE MARINADE
3 cloves garlic, crushed

120ml (4fl oz) soy sauce

120ml (4fl oz) sweet cider

4 tablespoons finely chopped
spring onions

1 teaspoon crushed fennel seed

1 tablespoon tomato purée

2 tablespoons clear honey

freshly ground black pepper

1 Mix together the marinade ingredients, add the venison ribs and leave in a cool place for 24 hours.

2 Remove the ribs from the marinade and grill on a barbecue for 8 minutes either side.

3 Put the marinade into a saucepan, bring to the boil and simmer for 4 minutes. Add the cornflour paste and sour cream and simmer for a further 3 minutes to make a thick creamy garlic sauce to serve with the ribs.

4 Serve the ribs with warm bread to dip into the sauce.

Sophia's Choice

✦ SERVES **4** ✦

The day my contract arrived from the publishers, Sophia Sanchez, the grand-daughter of a very close friend, came into the world. We celebrated the following week with a barbecue, and this recipe was created.

4 × 255g (9oz) venison steaks

FOR THE MARINADE
150ml (5fl oz) claret
2 garlic cloves, crushed
2 tablespoons clear honey

2 tablespoons English mustard
2 shallots, chopped
1 teaspoon mild curry powder
1 teaspoon celery salt
4 tablespoons sesame oil
1 tablespoon crushed almonds
freshly ground black pepper

1 Mix all the marinade ingredients together in a bowl.

2 Coat each steak all over with the marinade and lay them on a deep plate. Cover them with the remaining marinade and place in a cool place for 24 hours, turning the steaks occasionally.

3 Barbecue for 4 minutes either side, basting with the marinade. Serve with redcurrant jelly, baked potatoes and a fresh tomato salad with lots and lots of good claret.

Venison Steaks with Garlic and Five-Spice

✦ **SERVES 4** ✦

Five-spice powder gives an aromatic flavour to the venison.

6 × 225g (8oz) slices of venison haunch, trimmed

6 black peppercorns, crushed

12 shallots, sliced

4 slices of rindless streaky bacon, chopped

8 juniper berries

6 garlic cloves, crushed

3 tablespoons Pernod

4 teaspoons five-spice powder

4 tablespoons port

150ml (5fl oz) red wine

salt and freshly ground black pepper

25g (1oz) butter

2 tablespoons walnut oil

25g (1oz) flour

walnuts, to garnish

2 tablespoons chopped fresh coriander

1 Place the venison slices in a large deep roasting tray. Add the peppercorns, shallots, bacon, juniper berries, garlic, Pernod, five-spice powder, port and wine. Season well with salt and pepper. Leave to marinate in the refrigerator for 48 hours.

2 Preheat the oven to 180°C/350°F/gas 4. Remove the steaks from the marinade and fry them quickly in a large frying pan with the melted butter and walnut oil for 4 minutes either side. Put the steaks back into the marinade (reserving the juices in the frying pan) and bake in the oven, covered with foil, for 40 minutes. Remove the steaks to a warm serving dish. Sprinkle the flour over the juices in the frying pan and cook for 4 minutes, then add the marinade and bring to the boil. Simmer for 10 minutes, until the sauce is smooth. Pour the sauce over the venison steaks and garnish with walnuts and fresh coriander.

Oven-Baked Venison Steaks with Mustard

✦ **SERVES 4** ✦

*This is quick and simple. You can add a few of your favourite herbs to the coating mix,
and use different varieties of sherry or wine.*

4 × 225g (8oz) venison steaks	**2 tablespoons Dijon mustard**
1 tablespoon pink peppercorns	**2 tablespoons English mustard**
8 shallots, sliced	**2 tablespoons dry sherry**
2 tablespoons honey	**or white wine**
8 tablespoons double cream	**salt and freshly ground black pepper**

1 Preheat the oven to 200°C/400°F/gas 6.

2 Quickly seal the steaks on either side in a hot frying pan and place them on a baking tray.

3 Mix all the remaining ingredients together in a bowl and thoroughly coat the steaks. Bake in the preheated oven for 20 minutes.

4 Serve with a fresh watercress salad.

Baked Venison Cutlets with Oyster Mushrooms

✦ SERVES **4** ✦

Oyster mushrooms are now available all year round in supermarkets.

75g (3oz) butter	8 black peppercorns
4 × 285g (10oz) venison cutlets, trimmed	1 tablespoon sesame seeds
1 large onion, sliced	2 large tomatoes, halved
2 apples, peeled, cored and sliced	salt and freshly ground black pepper
285g (10oz) oyster mushrooms, sliced	fresh coriander leaves, to garnish
1 tablespoon chopped fresh coriander	Game Chips (page 149), to serve

1 Preheat the oven to 150°C/300°F/gas 2.

2 Melt 50g (2oz) of the butter in a large frying pan and gently fry the cutlets for 8 minutes on each side. Remove the cutlets from the pan and keep them warm in the oven.

3 Add the onion and apple slices to the frying pan and cook gently until slightly browned. Put the apples and onion on a serving dish, put the cutlets on top, and return to the oven to keep warm.

4 Add the remaining butter to the pan with the mushrooms, coriander and peppercorns. Cook for 3 minutes, then sprinkle with the sesame seeds. Add the mushrooms, peppercorns and juices to the cutlets, place the tomatoes around the edge, and return the dish to the oven for a further 10 minutes.

5 Season the cutlets well with salt and pepper and garnish with coriander leaves. Serve with game chips.

Casserole of Venison and Rabbit County Wicklow Style

✦ **SERVES 4** ✦

An Irish recipe for venison with rabbit.

100g (4oz) rindless streaky bacon

450g (1lb) boneless rabbit, chopped

450g (1lb) venison fillet, diced

4 potatoes, chopped

3 onions, sliced

2 carrots, sliced

100g (4oz) mushrooms, quartered

1 teaspoon chopped fresh thyme and parsley

salt and freshly ground black pepper

600ml (1 pint) chicken stock

1 tablespoon cornflour blended with a little wine

1 Preheat the oven to 180°C/350°F/gas 4.

2 Trim the bacon, cutting each rasher into 5 or 6 pieces.

3 Layer the rabbit, venison, bacon and vegetables in a casserole. Sprinkle with the herbs, and season well with salt and pepper. Pour over the stock and cook in the preheated oven for 90 minutes.

4 Thicken the casserole with the cornflour and wine mixture, and serve with red cabbage and rustic bread.

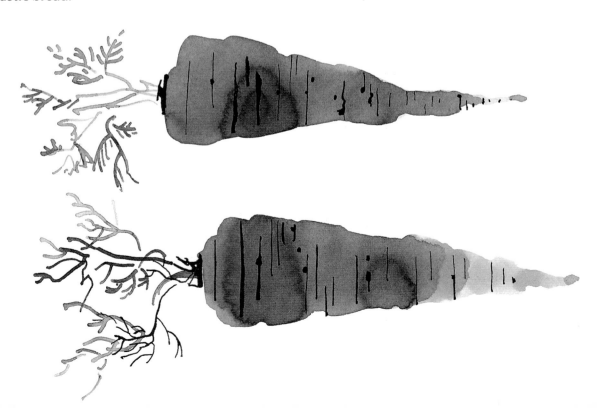

Traditional Scottish Venison Hotpot

✦ Serves 4 ✦

Another regional recipe, this time from Scotland.

50g (2oz) dripping	100g (4oz) lamb's kidney, diced
900g (2lb) venison rump, diced	225g (8oz) button mushrooms
2 large onions, sliced	10 oysters, shells removed
25g (1oz) plain flour	900g (2lb) potatoes, thinly sliced
600ml (1 pint) chicken stock	Game Chips (page 149), to serve
salt and freshly ground black pepper	

1 Heat the dripping in a large frying pan and quickly brown the diced venison. Remove the venison to a large ovenproof casserole with a lid and keep it warm in a low oven.

2 Fry the onions for about 3 minutes until they are transparent. Add the flour and cook for 2 minutes, then slowly add the chicken stock and season well, stirring all the time.

3 Remove the casserole from the oven. Preheat the oven to 190°C/375°F/gas 5. Add the kidney, mushrooms and oysters to the venison, layering them with the potatoes.

4 Pour over the onion stock and cook in the centre of the preheated oven for 2 hours. Take off the lid during the last 15 minutes to brown the potatoes.

5 Serve with game chips.

Venison Burgers

✦ Makes about 9 burgers ✦

Venison has a strong taste, which is made milder by including some pork sausagemeat in the minced mixture.

900g (2lb) minced venison	1 nutmeg, grated
2 onions, finely diced	plain flour
225g (8oz) pork sausagemeat	vegetable oil for frying
100g (4oz) fresh breadcrumbs, seasoned	

1 Blend together the venison, onions, sausagemeat, breadcrumbs and nutmeg. Form into about 9 burger shapes, coat with a little flour, and refrigerate until ready to cook them.

2 Gently heat a little oil and fry the burgers for 10 minutes on each side.

3 Serve with plum or tomato sauce and a crisp tomato salad.

Venison Bolognese

✦ SERVES **4** ✦

You can use this sauce for lasagne, cannelloni and other types of pasta.

2 tablespoons olive oil	150ml (5fl oz) Marsala
2 garlic cloves, crushed	1 × 400g (14oz) tin of chopped tomatoes
1 large onion, finely chopped	1 tablespoon chopped fresh basil
1 carrot, diced	2 tablespoons tomato purée
225g (8oz) minced venison	salt and freshly ground black pepper
75g (3oz) venison livers, chopped small	450g (1lb) spaghetti
100g (4oz) lean Parma ham, diced	

1 Heat the olive oil in a large saucepan and cook the garlic, onion and carrot for 6 minutes. Add the venison, livers and ham, and cook slowly for 12 minutes, browning the meat on all sides.

2 Add the wine, tomatoes, basil and tomato purée to the pan and cook, stirring, for 4 minutes. Season with salt and pepper, put a lid on the pan and simmer for 40 minutes. Remove the lid, stir and simmer for a further 15 minutes.

3 Cook the spaghetti in salted boiling water for 12 minutes or until *al dente*, drain and serve with the sauce.

WILD BOAR

Wild boar is a dense-textured, robustly flavoured dark red meat which is rich in protein but low in fat and cholesterol. It used to be a firm favourite of royals and aristocrats before it was hunted to extinction in Britain some 300 years ago, a traditional Christmas emblem being the boar's head boned, cooked and stuffed and brought to the table garlanded with holly.

Endemic to Europe, North Africa and parts of west and central Asia, wild boar is a fierce and wily game animal still abundant in many areas outside the UK, including the more mountainous regions of Spain, where owners of large estates used to organize a cowboy-style wild boar hunt with the villagers chasing on foot with sticks.

The firm of Barrow Boar, based in Somerset (see Useful Addresses, page 155), is managed by two friends of mine, Nigel Dauncey and animal scientist Christina Baskerville. In 1984 Nigel introduced French and Polish wild boar to the family farm, and now it is once again established in the ancient Somerset landscape. In addition to farm-reared wild boar meat and wild boar sausages with herbs or juniper berries, Barrow Boar offer a selection of exotic wild meats from around the world. The meat is derived from wild animals farmed extensively, and there is no depletion of wildlife stocks.

The French are great lovers of wild boar meat, and British chefs like to use it too. Cutlets, loin, noisettes and quarters of young wild boar can be cooked using any of the venison recipes on pages 80–90. Eldon Blue Pork is a tasty traditional pork, highly commended by Albert Roux. Male wild boars from Forsters Farm are crossed with Hampen gilts to give offspring closely resembling the Hampshire hog that once roamed the New Forest.

Spit-roast Loin of Eldon Blue Pork

✦ SERVES 4 ✦

This is a very simple dish – if you don't have a spit you can cut the pork into bite-size pieces and thread them on to kebab skewers.

900g (2lb) loin of Eldon Blue Pork, boned and rolled	**3 garlic cloves**
	salt and freshly ground black pepper
1 litre (1¾ pints) Portuguese red wine	**vegetable oil**

1 Place the pork in a deep dish with the wine and the garlic. Season with salt and pepper, then let it marinate for 6 hours. Turn it frequently.

2 Remove the loin from the marinade and place on the spit, making sure it is evenly balanced otherwise the spit will not turn. Let the spit turn slowly and cook for 90 minutes, basting all the time with the marinade and oil.

3 Alternatively roast in the oven at 200°C/400°F/gas 6 for 1 hour, then raise the heat to 230°C/450°F/gas 8 for 15 minutes.

Spanish Wild Boar Kebabs

✦ **SERVES 4** ✦

This dish is so simple, yet delicious. It is perfect for a summer barbecue with friends.

900g (2lb) wild boar steak	1 green pepper
225g (8oz) button mushrooms	2 large apples
225g (8oz) button onions or shallots	marinade (page 139)
1 red pepper	

1 Cut all the ingredients into bite-sized pieces and put into a dish. Cover with the marinade and refrigerate overnight.

2 Drain, reserving the marinade, then thread all the ingredients on to large bamboo skewers, placing a piece of steak after each mushroom, onion, pepper and piece of apple.

3 Cook on the barbecue for 5 minutes each side until tender, brushing with the reserved marinade.

English Eldon Blue Pork Kebabs with English Mustard

✦ **SERVES 4** ✦

Serve these kebabs on a bed of crisp ratatouille.

450g (1lb) Eldon Blue Pork fillet	100g (4oz) fresh pineapple
20 cherry tomatoes	1 green pepper
100g (4oz) button mushrooms	4 tablespoons English mustard

1 Cut all the ingredients into bite-sized pieces and thread them on to bamboo skewers. Brush them with the mustard and cook on the barbecue for 20–25 minutes, turning and basting with a little more mustard blended with the juice from the pineapple.

Roast Loin of Eldon Blue Pork
with Bordelaise Sauce

✦ **SERVES 4–6** ✦

I love pork crackling, and to make perfect crackling you must score it evenly. It is simple – all you do is to penetrate the skin and a little of the fat below it with a very sharp knife, making diamond shape cuts about 1cm (½ inch) apart. Gently brush the pork with a little oil, and salt it generously all over.

1–2.8kg (2–6lb) loin of Eldon Blue Pork	coarse salt
salt and freshly ground black pepper	honey
bay leaves	Bordelaise Sauce (page 144)
fresh rosemary	Game Chips (page 149)

1 Preheat the oven to 230°C/450°F/gas 8.

2 To get the crackling *really* crisp, place the joint skin side down in a roasting tin and pour in about 2cm (1 inch) of boiling water. Place the tin in the centre of the preheated oven and cook for 20 minutes. Remove the tin, pour off the liquid and keep it for basting the pork. Put the pork back into the roasting tin skin side up and season, adding a few bay leaves and pressing some rosemary into the score marks.

3 Reduce the heat to 180°C/350°F/gas 4 and cook for 30 minutes per 450g (1lb), basting every 20 minutes. Allow the pork to cool then remove the crackling and cut into long thin strips. Put the strips on a baking tray, sprinkle with coarse salt, coat with a little honey, and cook for a further 10 minutes.

4 Serve with piping hot Bordelaise sauce, game chips and apple sauce.

Carbonnade of Wild Boar with Guinness

✦ SERVES 4 ✦

This is a typical recipe from Normandy. The French used red wine and I decided to substitute Guinness, adding juniper berries and the sweetness of the parsnip.

900g (2lb) wild boar steak	225g (8oz) button mushrooms
salt and freshly ground black pepper	225g (8oz) parsnip, diced
2 tablespoons olive oil	2 tablespoons juniper berries
25g (1oz) butter	1 × 270ml bottle of Guinness
450g (1lb) shallots	150ml (5fl oz) Espagnole Sauce (page 143)
1 tablespoon flour	2 tablespoons redcurrant jelly

1 Season the meat with salt and pepper. Heat the olive oil in a frying pan and brown the meat all over, then transfer it to an ovenproof casserole.

2 Add the butter to the frying pan and sauté the shallots, stirring constantly, until they are golden brown. Sprinkle with flour, stir well, and add to the casserole. Add the mushrooms, parsnip, juniper berries, Guinness and Espagnole sauce and cook over a low heat for 2 hours. Taste for seasoning and finally stir in the redcurrant jelly.

Wild Boar Risotto

✦ SERVES 4 ✦

This famous dish is known throughout the world and it is perhaps the best known of all Italian risottos.

100g (4oz) butter	150ml (5fl oz) white wine
50g (2oz) beef marrow, chopped	1 teaspoon crumbled saffron
1 large onion, chopped	salt and freshly ground black pepper
175g (6oz) wild boar steak, minced	175g (6oz) grated Parmesan cheese
450g (1lb) Italian rice	50g (2oz) butter, melted
600ml (1 pint) hot Game Stock (page 141)	

1 Heat 50g (2oz) of the butter and the beef marrow in a deep frying pan. Add the chopped onion and minced meat and cook until golden brown. Add the rice and stir well. Cook for 15 minutes, then add the hot stock, white wine, saffron, salt and pepper, and mix well. Simmer gently for 20 minutes, stirring occasionally.

2 Taste the rice and add a little more stock if necessary, then simmer for a further 10 minutes. Just before serving, sprinkle with the grated Parmesan cheese and pour the melted butter over.

Thai Stir-Fried Eldon Blue Pork with Pasta and Vegetables

✦ SERVES 4 ✦

I like to use tagliolini for this recipe.

3 tablespoons sesame oil	1 green chilli, finely chopped
340g (12oz) Eldon Blue Pork fillet, thinly sliced	1 red pepper, thinly sliced
salt and freshly ground black pepper	1 green pepper, thinly sliced
450g (1lb) pasta	3 courgettes, thinly sliced
8 shallots, sliced	2 tablespoons ground almonds
2 garlic cloves, finely chopped	1 teaspoon ground cinnamon
2.5cm (1 inch) fresh ginger, peeled and grated	1 tablespoon oyster sauce
	50g (2oz) creamed coconut, grated

1 Heat the sesame oil in a wok. Season the meat with salt and pepper and stir-fry for 8 minutes.

2 Meanwhile cook the pasta in boiling salted water until *al dente*.

3 Add the shallots, garlic, ginger and chilli to the meat in the wok and cook for 2 minutes. Add the peppers and courgettes and cook for 1 minute. Finally add the ground almonds, cinnamon, oyster sauce and coconut, stir-fry for 1 minute and serve immediately with the pasta.

Wild Boar Curry with Lime and Rosemary

✦ SERVES 6–8 ✦

The flavour of the lime and chillies combined with the rosemary gives this curry a very unique taste.

4 tablespoons groundnut oil	4 tomatoes, chopped
2 large onions, finely chopped	1 teaspoon rosemary
900g (2lb) wild boar steak, diced	1 teaspoon garam masala
50g (2oz) seasoned flour	300ml (10fl oz) Game Stock (page 141)
8 shallots, peeled	2 tablespoons Worcestershire sauce
4 garlic cloves, crushed with a	3 tablespoons hot curry paste
little olive oil	salt and freshly ground black pepper
juice and zest of 1 lime	1 sprig of fresh rosemary
2 green chillies, finely chopped	150ml (5fl oz) fromage frais
3 large potatoes, diced	

1 Preheat the oven to 180°C/350°F/gas 4.

2 Heat the oil in a large frying pan. Coat the onions and meat in the seasoned flour and cook for about 6 minutes, browning the meat all over. Put the onions and meat in a large deep casserole. Slowly fry the shallots in the same pan, adding the crushed garlic, lime juice and zest, chillies, potatoes, tomatoes, rosemary and garam masala. Add the stock, Worcestershire sauce and hot curry paste and season with salt and pepper, finally adding the sprig of rosemary.

3 Pour the sauce over the steak and cover the casserole with a lid or foil. Cook in the centre of the preheated oven for 2 hours until the meat is very tender. Remove the sprig of rosemary, add the fromage frais, and cook for a further 10 minutes. Serve with rice.

Wild Boar Sausage Pot with Paprika

✦ SERVES **4** ✦

This is a Polish dish traditionally served with cabbage and baby beetroot.

550g (20oz) wild boar sausages	225ml (8fl oz) Demi-glace Sauce (page 143)
450g (1lb) onions, sliced	3 tablespoons tomato purée
3 tablespoons olive oil	2 tablespoons paprika
25g (1oz) butter	1 teaspoon dried marjoram
225g (8oz) button mushrooms	1 teaspoon German mustard
1 red pepper, chopped	6 tablespoons sour cream
1 green pepper, chopped	salt and freshly ground black pepper
8 tomatoes, chopped	

1 Slice the sausages into bite-sized chunks and fry them with the onions in the olive oil and butter for 4 minutes. Add the mushrooms, peppers and tomatoes and continue frying for a further 3 minutes. Pour on the demi-glace sauce and add the tomato purée, paprika, marjoram and mustard. Bring to the boil and simmer for 1 hour.

2 Add the sour cream and gently heat through, seasoning with salt and pepper.

SOMETHING FISHY

*T*he British are a nation of anglers, yet fish is not often included in books about game. The usual game fish are salmon and trout. Fish is at its best straight from the water, so the ideal is to catch it yourself or obtain it straight from the angler.

Fish you buy at a supermarket counter is likely to have been frozen before sale. The same applies to fish at a fishmonger's and it is best to check before buying. A really fresh fish will have a mild, salty smell. The fish you buy is likely to be ready to cook, but here is the procedure for those who catch their own fish or buy them just caught.

CLEANING, BONING AND FILLETING

Using a sharp knife, cut the fish open lengthways. Remove all the innards and cut away the gills. Wash well under cold running water to remove any blood.

To bone the fish, first clean it, then cut off the head and tail. Open the fish out flat, flesh side down, and press firmly along the backbone to loosen it. Turn the fish over and you should be able to remove the bone easily.

Clean the fish and cut off the head. It is now ready for filleting. Make a crossways cut just above the tail, and then gradually slice the flesh away, keeping the knife blade flat. Turn over and repeat with the other side of the fish.

SALMON

The salmon is spawned in fresh water but spends part of its life at sea. The female salmon lays her eggs in a quiet part of the river or stream, and covers them in gravel until they hatch. When the baby salmon are about eighteen months they make their way out to sea, where they can remain for anything up to five years.

When the mature salmon is ready to spawn, it returns to the river of its birth, and it is at this point that many salmon are caught commercially. If it escapes the fishing boats, it will begin to make its way upriver and at that point may be caught by an angler with rod and line.

A young salmon a year or so old will weigh up to 1.8kg (4lb), and a four-year-old fish returning to spawn will be about 3–6.8kg (7–15lb). It is a healthy food, being low in fat and cholesterol.

Salmon can be cooked in many delicious ways: it can be poached, steamed, baked, grilled or smoked for a lovely, delicate flavour. A whole poached salmon is a special occasion dish, either hot or cold. It can also be made into pâtés and terrines.

Kipper Salmon (Smoked Salmon)

✦ SERVES 4 ✦

I have taken this recipe from The Scots Kitchen *by F. Marian McNeill, first published in 1929 by Blackie. I have never seen it in any other cookery book. Kippered salmon was mentioned in the Household Book of James V (1513–42). Today you can buy home smokers with hickory, oak or fruitwood chips. For this recipe, pour a little whisky or rum over the chips and let them dry for 2 days. This recipe sounds a lengthy process, but it is well worth the effort to make your own smoked salmon. I have adapted the recipe slightly – the original uses herring-salt, which I have changed to sea salt. This method can also be used for smoking trout and for other game, such as venison.*

1 fresh wild salmon	**whisky**
sea salt	**oak chips, soaked in whisky and**
olive oil	**allowed to dry for 2 days**
demerara sugar	

1 Cut the salmon in half lengthways, remove the backbone and any excess bones, and wipe the fish carefully with a dry cloth. Lay the halves of salmon side by side on a wooden cutting board and cover all over with the sea salt. Leave for 24 hours.

2 Wipe off the surplus salt and hang the two halves of salmon in a cool area of the kitchen for 6 hours, with a bowl underneath to catch the juices.

3 Put the salmon halves on the cutting board again and completely cover with olive oil. Leave for another 6 hours.

4 Drain the oil from the salmon and rub off the excess with a cloth soaked in whisky. Cover the salmon all over with demerara sugar and leave for a further 24 hours. (This removes the salt and helps to cure the salmon.)

5 Wipe off the sugar and hang the fish again to drain. Treat once more with the olive oil cure for 6 hours, then wipe off again with the cloth soaked in whisky and the salmon is now ready for smoking.

6 The smoker should be set with oak chips soaked in whisky and allowed to dry, and then lit on two occasions, leaving the fish to mature in between. Follow the instructions given with your home smoker.

It is a lengthy process spread over 3 days, and a costly method of smoking, but the sweet cured and smoked flavour is not something you can purchase in a supermarket!

Wild Salmon Steaks in Foil

✦ SERVES 4 ✦

You can add almost any combination of your favourite herbs, butters and oils to create your own version of this recipe.

4 salmon steaks	**salt and freshly ground black pepper**
100g (4oz) unsalted butter, plus extra for greasing	**4 tablespoons chopped parsley**
	4 tablespoons chopped chives
4 tablespoons lemon juice	**sour cream, parsley sprigs and snipped**
4 tablespoons lime juice	**chives, to garnish**

1 Place the salmon steaks on individual pieces of buttered cooking foil big enough to completely enclose the fish. Put 25g (1oz) of butter on each salmon steak. Divide the rest of the ingredients between the salmon steaks.

2 Wrap the steaks up in the foil, sealing them completely. Place the fish in the fridge for 3 hours.

3 Bake the fish, still wrapped in the foil, on a barbecue for 25 minutes until the salmon is tender. Carefully open the foil and remove the salmon on to individual plates, reserving the juices in the foil. Remove the outer skin around each salmon steak, and the central bone if it comes away easily.

4 Pour over the fish juices and serve garnished with a little sour cream, sprigs of fresh parsley and snipped fresh chives.

Freshly Poached Wild Salmon in Aspic with Freshwater Prawn and Asparagus Salad

✦ SERVES 4 ✦

This is a dish for a special occasion, made more luxurious by serving with a delicious seafood salad.

1 × 2.3kg (5lb) salmon, gutted, head and tail left on	**FOR THE FRESHWATER PRAWN AND ASPARAGUS SALAD**
1 litre (2 pints) Court-Bouillon (page 142)	1 lollo rosso lettuce
1 egg white, plus the egg shell	1 oak leaf lettuce
2 tablespoons gelatine	1 head of radicchio
1 cucumber	olive oil
1 red pepper	lemon juice
3 tomatoes	salt and freshly ground black pepper
2 lemons	1 bunch of fresh asparagus, trimmed and cooked
	450g (1lb) large freshwater prawns
	1 lemon, cut in slices, to serve

1 Preheat the oven to 180°C/350°F/gas 4.

2 Line a baking tin with cooking foil, ensuring that the foil is overhanging the edge on two sides. Place the salmon carefully on to the foil on its side and strain over the court-bouillon. Cover with foil and bake in the preheated oven for 45 minutes.

3 Remove the foil from the top of the baking tin and allow the salmon to cool naturally for 2 hours. Carefully lift the foil from the tray, removing the salmon with it. Peel off the skin and place the salmon on a large serving dish. Refrigerate.

4 Meanwhile strain the court-bouillon into another saucepan. Boil to reduce by half, then add the egg white and shell, let it simmer for 5 minutes to clarify, and strain the court-bouillon through a very fine sieve.

5 Soften the gelatine according to the instructions on the packet and add to the court-bouillon to make the aspic. Allow it to cool slightly and then brush the salmon with the aspic, coating it every 5 minutes for 20 minutes. Decorate with slices of cucumber, red pepper, tomato and lemon, give it a final coat of aspic, and serve with the Prawn and Asparagus Salad.

6 To make the salad, wash the three lettuces and tear them into pieces. Sprinkle them generously with olive oil and lemon juice and season with salt and freshly ground black pepper. Arrange them on a serving dish.

7 Place the asparagus into a fan shape on top of the lettuce, surround it with the prawns and slices of lemon.

Poached Salmon with Orange and Basil Sauce

✦ SERVES 4 ✦

Orange and basil are two of my favourite flavours, but you can choose your own. Try lime with tarragon!

4 wild salmon steaks	**FOR THE ORANGE AND BASIL SAUCE**
50g (2oz) butter	**25g (1oz) butter**
175ml (6fl oz) Court-Bouillon (page 142)	**25g (1oz) flour**
a pinch of sea salt	**150ml (¼ pint) warm milk**
8 peppercorns	**150ml (5fl oz) fresh orange juice**
1 sprig of dill	**4 tablespoons orange curaçao**
1 sprig of basil	**juice and zest of 3 oranges**
2 oranges, sliced	**50g (2oz) chopped fresh basil**
sprigs of fresh basil	**1 tablespoon honey**
1 bunch of watercress	**salt and freshly ground black pepper**

1 Add the salmon steaks to a large non-stick pan with the butter, court-bouillon, salt, peppercorns, dill, basil and half the orange slices. Bring to the boil, reduce the heat and simmer for 10 minutes with a lid on. Using a fish slice, carefully remove the salmon to a plate. Reserve the court-bouillon.

2 Take off the skin of the salmon and remove the centre bone. Arrange on a warm serving dish, cover with a little greased foil and put in the oven to keep warm.

3 To make the sauce, melt the butter in a saucepan, add the flour and cook for 2 minutes. Slowly add the warm milk and strain in about 100ml (4fl oz) of the reserved court-bouillon. Add the orange juice, curaçao and zest and simmer for a further 12 minutes, stirring constantly.

4 Finally add the basil and honey, stir gently, and season with salt and freshly ground black pepper. Simmer for 5 minutes more, then pour the sauce over the salmon and serve, garnished with the remaining slices of orange, fresh basil and watercress.

Wild Salmon Fillets Filled with Leek and Parsley

✦ SERVES 4 ✦

A variation on the usual plainly cooked salmon fillets.

4 × 175g (6oz) salmon fillets

salt and freshly ground black pepper

150ml (5fl oz) sesame oil

FOR THE SALMON FILLING
285g (10oz) salmon tail, minced

100g (4oz) leeks, finely chopped

2 sprigs of parsley, finely chopped

2 garlic cloves, crushed with a little sesame oil

salt and freshly ground black pepper

1 Cut a pocket into the side of each salmon fillet, seasoning the fish well on the inside and outside.

2 Mix the filling ingredients together and fill each pocket with equal amounts of the filling. Heat the sesame oil gently in a deep frying pan and gently fry the salmon fillets on each side until cooked.

Wild Salmon and Tuna Fishcakes

✦ **SERVES 4** ✦

*One of my favourite chefs, Rick Stein, whose restaurant in Padstow, Cornwall, features the pride
of modern British cuisine – the humble fishcake – remembers them being made of pollack and mackerel.
Here is my recipe using wild salmon fillet and tuna steak.*

450g (1lb) wild salmon fillet, skin and
any excess bones removed

450g (1lb) tuna or swordfish, skin and
any excess bones removed

3 eggs, beaten

1 tablespoon English mustard

1 tablespoon Worcestershire sauce

450g (1lb) cooked mashed potato

175g (6oz) breadcrumbs

50ml (2fl oz) double cream

salt and freshly ground black pepper

flour for dusting

sunflower oil for frying

1 Flake the raw fish and add to the eggs, mustard, Worcestershire sauce, mashed potato, breadcrumbs, cream and seasoning. Mix thoroughly, either by hand or in a blender. With floured hands, shape the mixture into fishcake shapes about 2.5cm (1 inch) thick and about 7cm (3 inches) wide.

2 Preheat the oven to 200°C/400°F/gas 6.

3 Place the fish cakes into hot oil and fry them for 4–5 minutes until golden brown on both sides. Drain them on kitchen paper and put them in the preheated oven for 10 minutes.

4 Serve the fishcakes with a home-made mustard or tartare sauce or tomato ketchup.

TROUT

There are several species of trout, but the usual game trout are the native brown trout, which is found throughout the British Isles, and the rainbow trout which is bred for stocking lakes and reservoirs. Salmon trout, with pink flesh tasting rather like salmon, are also farmed in large numbers.

Small fresh trout are best sautéed in butter, perhaps with a sprinkling of almonds or herbs. The famous French dish *truite au bleu* is simply trout dipped in vinegar, then simmered in a court-bouillon (page 142).

Freshwater rainbow trout weighs around 1kg (2lb).

Wild Trout with Almonds, Apples and Smoked Bacon

✦ **SERVES 4** ✦

I have a neighbour who goes fishing all the time, and he brings me back some trout on nearly every trip. The flavour of wild trout is far superior to that of farmed. This is an excellent recipe for the barbecue. Try to get really good smoked bacon — Welsh and Northern Irish curers have some of the finest smoked bacon in Europe.

4 wild trout, gutted and cleaned	12 slices of rindless smoked streaky bacon
salt and freshly ground black pepper	25g (1oz) butter
2 apples, peeled, cored and sliced	2 apples, cored and sliced
100g (4oz) chopped almonds	4 sprigs of freshly washed mint
4 sprigs of mint	25g (1oz) chopped almonds
juice of 1 lemon	

1 Preheat the oven to 200°C/400°F/gas 6.

2 Open up the cavity of each trout and wash through thoroughly with warm salt water. Season each cavity with salt and freshly ground black pepper. Put equal amounts of sliced apple and chopped almonds into each cavity, and add a sprig of mint to each. Squeeze over the juice of the lemon. Carefully cover the whole of the trout except the head and tail with three slices of smoked bacon, arranging the bacon in a spiral.

3 Grease a deep baking tray with the butter and put in the trout, with the loose ends of bacon underneath. Season with more freshly ground black pepper and bake for 20 minutes in the preheated oven, turning the trout over after 10 minutes.

4 Remove the fish to a serving dish and serve garnished with sliced apple, fresh mint sprigs and chopped almonds.

Wild Trout Fillets with Bacon and Almond Sauce

✦ **SERVES 4** ✦

Wild trout has a completely different flavour from farmed or river trout, and I recommend that you try it.

4 wild trout fillets, skin and bones removed

FOR THE SAUCE

25g (1oz) butter

4 shallots, chopped

100g (4oz) rindless smoked streaky bacon, diced

2 tablespoons almonds

10 cardamom pods

2 whole star anise

1 tablespoon coriander seeds, crushed

salt and freshly ground black pepper

150ml (5fl oz) white wine

150ml (5fl oz) Court-bouillon (page 142)

150ml (5fl oz) double cream or fromage frais

juice of 1 lemon

lemon slices to garnish

1 Melt the butter in a pan and cook the shallots, bacon and almonds for 4 minutes. Add the spices and seasoning and cook for a further 3 minutes.

2 Add the wine and court-bouillon, and boil to reduce the sauce by half. Add the cream and reduce again by half. Grill the trout fillets for 4 minutes and place on to a serving dish. Keep warm. Season well with salt and pepper and finish with the lemon juice. Pour the sauce over the trout and garnish with fresh slices of lemon.

Soups

oup has always been a very important part of the British diet. In Mrs Beeton's day, dinner, being the main meal of the day, was a matter of considerable importance, and, as she wrote in All About Cookery, 'a well-served table is a striking index of human ingenuity and resource'. Every dinner in Mrs Beeton's time started with some form of soup or broth. The Prince Regent loved game soup, but started his meals with caviar and finished with Rosa Lewis's famous Quail Pudding (see page 41).

Soup can be made from almost any ingredient: meat, fish, vegetables, even fruit. It can be clear, like a consommé, or thickened by puréeing or by adding rice or flour. Peasant soups in many countries contain bread. Soup is usually thought of as a warming dish, but some soups are meant to be served cold. Soup is probably the most adaptable meal there is.

Soup can be served as a first course or snack, and if it is substantial enough it will make a main meal with crusty bread and perhaps a salad. It can be transported easily in a vacuum flask, and makes perfect picnic food.

The basis of any good soup is stock, which is made by slowly simmering bones, flavouring vegetables and seasonings in water. In France stock is known as fond, *in other words 'foundation'. On pages 141-2 you will find recipes for game stocks, which will form the foundation of the delicious game soups in this chapter.*

Game Consommé

✦ SERVES 8–10 ✦

Really good game stock will make really good consommé.

1.75 litres (3 pints) Game Stock (page 141)	whites of 4 eggs, plus shells
150ml (5fl oz) medium sherry	salt and freshly ground black pepper

1 Put the stock and sherry into a large saucepan and heat gently for 5 minutes.

2 Add the whites of egg and the shells, and whisk until the mixture begins to boil. When the mixture boils, remove the pan from the heat and leave to stand for 10 minutes. Repeat this process 3 times. This allows the egg white to trap the sediment and clarify the soup.

3 Let the consommé cool for 5 minutes. Carefully place a piece of fine muslin over a clean saucepan. Strain the soup through the muslin into the saucepan, and repeat this process twice. Gently reheat the consommé, season, taste and serve. Add a little cooked diced game if you like.

Cream of Game Soup

✦ SERVES 4 ✦

For Hubert Lowrey and Pete Vickers.

50g (2oz) unsalted butter	pinch of bicarbonate of soda
1 large onion, peeled and chopped	salt and freshly ground black pepper
285g (10oz) cooked game, finely shredded	15ml (1 tablespoon) chopped basil
600ml (1 pint) Game Stock (page 141)	150ml (¼ pint) double cream
900g (2lb) firm tomatoes, skinned and roughly chopped	fresh basil leaves

1 Melt the butter in a large saucepan and fry the onion for 3 minutes. Add the cooked game and 300ml (½ pint) of the stock to the pan, with the chopped tomatoes and bicarbonate of soda. Bring to the boil and simmer for 20 minutes.

2 Allow to cool, then liquidize the soup, pouring it through a fine sieve back into the saucepan. Add the remainder of the stock and season with salt and pepper. Add the chopped basil and pour the soup into a tureen. Swirl the cream around the top of the soup, and garnish with fresh basil leaves.

3 Serve with deep-fried croûtons.

Scotland the Brave Giblet Soup

✦ **S**ERVES **4** ✦

I have always said nobody can make soups like the Scots. This is really a main course soup and was originally made with giblets, beef and chicken. You can add a little rice and some peppers to bring out the colour if you like.

25g (1oz) butter	1 bouquet garni
285g (10oz) game giblets	salt and freshly ground white pepper
350g (12oz) uncooked pheasant meat	8 prunes, stoned and halved
350g (12oz) leeks, cut into 2.5cm (1 inch) pieces	2 tablespoons uncooked rice (optional)
	1 green or red pepper, diced (optional)
1 litre (1¾ pints) Giblet Stock (page 142)	

1 Melt the butter in a large saucepan and fry the giblets, pheasant and leeks for 8 minutes. Add the stock and bouquet garni, seasoning well to taste.

2 Bring the soup to the boil and simmer for 90 minutes or until reduced by one-third. Add the prunes, with a little rice and diced peppers if you like, and simmer for 20 minutes.

Game Soup with Sherry

✦ SERVES 4 ✦

This recipe is served in most game shooting areas of the British Isles and is very popular with the golfing fraternity. For an extra boost, substitute fresh cranberry juice for half of the game stock.

50g (2oz) butter	50g (2oz) plain flour
1 onion, diced	1 litre (1¾ pints) Game Stock (page 141)
1 carrot, diced	1 bay leaf
1 celery stick, diced	8 black peppercorns
450g (1lb) diced venison, fat removed	pinch of salt
450g (1lb) chopped mixed game meat	3 tablespoons redcurrant jelly
(rabbit, pheasant or grouse)	150ml (¼ pint) of sweet sherry

1 Melt the butter in a large saucepan. Add the onion, carrot, celery and meat, cook slowly for 6 minutes, then sprinkle with flour. Cook for a further 2 minutes and slowly add the stock, bay leaf, peppercorns and salt and simmer for 1 hour. Add the redcurrant jelly and sherry and let the soup stand for at least 4 hours.

2 Remove the bay leaf and put the soup through a blender or liquidizer. Reheat, simmer for 10 minutes, then serve with croûtons.

Guinea Fowl and Vermicelli Soup

✦ SERVES 4 ✦

Guinea fowl is excellent for soup, milder in flavour than any other game, with the texture of chicken.

450g (1lb) guinea fowl meat, skin removed	sprinkling of mace
600ml (20fl oz) Game Stock (page 141)	150ml (5fl oz) double cream
1 small onion, chopped	15g (½oz) butter, softened
½ teaspoon salt	15g (½oz) flour
6 peppercorns	100g (4oz) vermicelli, cooked and
1 teaspoon cloves	kept warm

1 Put the guinea fowl meat and bones into a large saucepan and add the stock. Bring to the boil, add the onion, salt, peppercorns, cloves and mace, and allow to simmer gently for about 2 hours, until the liquid is reduced by one-third.

2 Strain the soup, skim off any fat, and remove any bones from the guinea fowl. Return the soup and meat to a clean saucepan.

3 Add the cream and bring to the boil slowly. Make a *beurre manié* by blending the softened butter and flour together, and stir into the soup to thicken it slightly.

4 Just before you are ready to serve the soup, add the cooked vermicelli.

Variation

For a quicker and simpler recipe, use 450g (1lb) quail meat instead of guinea fowl and simmer for 40 minutes.

Duck and Pea Soup

✦ **SERVES 4** ✦

*Peas and wild duckling are a perfect and traditional combination, though rare in soup
— it really is quite a surprising taste.*

3 slices of rindless smoked streaky bacon, diced	450g (1lb) ready-soaked peas
4 Gressingham duck breasts, skin removed and thinly sliced	2.3 litres (4 pints) chicken stock
1 large onion, chopped	salt and freshly ground black pepper
small knob of butter	150ml (5fl oz) double cream
	chopped parsley to garnish
	croûtons to serve

1 Put the bacon, duck meat and onion into a large saucepan with a little butter and cook over a gentle heat for 8 minutes.

2 Add the peas and stock to the pan, bring to the boil, season lightly with salt and pepper, then cover the pan and simmer for 2 hours.

3 Add the cream, stir well and blend thoroughly. Sprinkle with parsley and serve with cheesy croûtons.

Tom's Rabbit Soup

✦ SERVES **4** ✦

This recipe comes originally from a beautiful area of Moira in County Down, in the north of Ireland. For Kimberley Hughes, remembering Bolton market.

3 slices of rindless smoked streaky bacon, chopped	600ml (1 pint) Giblet Stock (page 142)
450g (1lb) boneless rabbit meat	600ml (1 pint) fresh milk
25g (1oz) butter	150ml (5fl oz) double cream
450g (1lb) King Edward potatoes, chopped	salt and freshly ground black pepper
450g (1lb) onions, chopped	freshly chopped parsley

1 Put the bacon and rabbit meat into a large saucepan and cook gently for 10 minutes. Add the butter, potatoes and onions and cook for 15 minutes, stirring all the time.

2 Add the stock and milk, bring to the boil and simmer for 45 minutes. Blend in the cream and simmer for 5 minutes, then season with salt and pepper, add the parsley and serve with Irish soda bread.

Venison Broth

✦ SERVES **4** ✦

A firm family favourite, this really is a taste of Scotland that you won't forget. The soup should be left for at least 2 days after making, before being reheated and served with oatmeal cakes or bread.

50g (2oz) presoaked dried peas	salt and freshly ground white pepper
900g (2lb) neck of venison, bones and fat removed, and diced	1 large carrot, diced
1 litre (2 pints) Game Stock (page 141)	1 small turnip, diced
600ml (1 pint) water	1 large leek, thinly sliced
50g (2oz) barley, washed	1 red onion, finely chopped

1 Put the dried peas and venison into a saucepan and add the stock and water. Bring slowly to the boil, skimming as necessary. When no more scum rises, add the washed barley and some salt. Simmer for 35 minutes.

2 Add the rest of the ingredients and simmer for 2 hours, skim the fat and then leave to stand for at least 24 hours.

3 Reheat, adjust the seasoning, and serve.

Wild Salmon Soup

✦ **SERVES 4** ✦

This is a perfect dinner party soup.

450g (1lb) wild salmon fillet, thinly sliced	225g (8oz) uncooked prawns, shells removed
600ml (1 pint) Fish Court-Bouillon (page 142)	25g (1oz) butter
600ml (1 pint) milk	4 tablespoons cream
450g (1lb) potatoes, cooked and sliced	chopped, fresh parsley to garnish
salt and freshly ground black pepper	

1 Put the salmon into a large saucepan, add the court-bouillon, and simmer for about 15 minutes. Remove the fish from the pan and take out any bones, returning the bones to the stock. Simmer for 10 minutes.

2 Flake the fish. Strain the stock carefully. Add the milk, potatoes and flaked fish and simmer for a further 10 minutes, adjusting the seasoning. Add the prawns, butter and cream and simmer for 5 minutes, then garnish with parsley and serve with crusty wholemeal bread.

Variation

For a more luxurious flavour try this recipe using smoked salmon ends (much cheaper than smoked salmon slices). Sprinkle with the smoked salmon and simmer for 10 minutes.

PIES, TERRINES AND PATES

This is probably my favourite section of the book. Pies are such a major part of British culinary tradition, even occurring in nursery rhymes! I love the old stories — 'four and twenty blackbirds baked in a pie', for example. Did it really happen?

Well, the answer is . . . yes and no. In 1813 Lord Talbot, the then Viceroy of Ireland, presented King George III with twenty-four woodcock baked in a pie. The custom continued, with the pie being sent to the reigning sovereign in England every Christmas. In 1929 such a pie was presented by James McNeill, Governor General of Ireland, to His Majesty King George V at Sandringham. So yes, it happened, but no, they weren't blackbirds!

I come from Lancashire, where pie-eating is part of the lifestyle. A famous north-country pie made for Sir Henry Grey in 1770 was sent to London by stage coach — it contained more than thirty-six different ingredients followed by 2 bushels of flour, 20lb of butter, 4 geese, 2 turkeys, 4 wild ducks, 2 woodcocks, 6 snipe, 4 partridges, 2 curlews and 6 pigeons. The completed pie weighed one and a half hundredweight.

Pies can be made with game bought specially for the purpose, or with oddments left over from another dish. They can be served hot or cold, which makes them ideal for buffet parties, and they make a good spread at the festive season. Chutneys, pickles, mustards and salads make delicious accompaniments.

In the Basics chapter on page 139 you will find recipes for several different types of pastry, ranging from the standard shortcrust to the hot-water crust pastry used for that splendid British institution, the pork pie. Each recipe will specify the pastry to use.

Pheasant and Wild Mushroom Pie with Two Pastries

✦ SERVES 4 ✦

This pie uses two pastries – a shortcrust base and a puff pastry topping.
The broccoli stalks are a surprise ingredient.

50g (2oz) butter	150ml (5fl oz) Giblet Gravy (page 142)
2 carrots, very finely diced	150ml (5fl oz) double cream
8 shallots, sliced	450g (1lb) pheasant breast, cooked
175g (6oz) rindless streaky bacon, chopped	and sliced
1 large cooking apple, cored and sliced	175g (6oz) wild mushrooms
4 juniper berries, crushed	50g (2oz) Cheddar cheese, grated
100g (4oz) thinly sliced broccoli stalks,	salt and freshly ground black pepper
blanched	175g (6oz) Shortcrust Pastry (page 152)
25g (1oz) plain flour	100g (4oz) Puff Pastry (page 153)
150ml (5fl oz) fresh milk, warmed	1 egg, beaten

1 Preheat the oven to 200°C/400°F/gas 6.

2 Melt the butter in a large saucepan and fry the carrots, shallots, bacon, apple, crushed juniper berries and broccoli stalks for about 8 minutes, stirring occasionally. Add the flour and cook for a further 2 minutes, then gradually add the warm milk, giblet gravy and cream, and stir continuously for about 6 minutes until the sauce becomes thick and creamy.

3 Add the pheasant, wild mushrooms and grated cheese to the sauce, seasoning well with salt and freshly ground black pepper. Allow the mixture to cool.

4 Roll out the shortcrust pastry and use to line a greased ovenproof pie dish. Pour in the cooled pheasant mixture. Top with puff pastry, brush with beaten egg and bake in the centre of the preheated oven for 30 minutes.

5 Serve with baked parsnips and creamed potatoes.

Pheasant and Mushroom Pie

✦ **SERVES 4** ✦

This recipe is from the south-east of England. In Wales they use leeks instead of mushrooms and in Ireland they use potatoes.

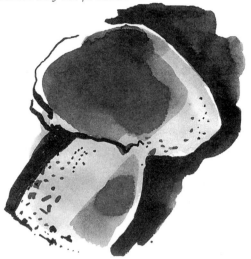

50g (2oz) butter	450g (1lb) pheasant breast, cooked and diced
2 carrots, very finely diced	
8 shallots, sliced	50g (2oz) Cheddar cheese, grated
225g (8oz) button mushrooms, sliced	salt and freshly ground black pepper
25g (1oz) plain flour	175g (6oz) Shortcrust Pastry (page 152)
300ml (10fl oz) fresh milk, warmed	100g (4oz) Puff Pastry (page 153)
150ml (5fl oz) double cream	1 egg, beaten, for glazing

1 Preheat the oven to 200°C/400°F/gas 6.

2 Melt the butter in a large saucepan and gently fry the carrots, shallots and mushrooms for about 10 minutes, stirring occasionally.

3 Add the flour and cook for a further 2 minutes. Gradually add the warm milk and the cream, stirring continuously until the sauce becomes thick and creamy.

4 Add the cooked pheasant breast and grated cheese to the sauce, season well with salt and freshly ground black pepper, and leave to cool.

5 Roll out the shortcrust pastry and use to line a greased ovenproof pie dish. Pour in the cooled pheasant mixture, top with a puff pastry lid, brush with beaten egg and bake in the centre of the oven for 30 minutes.

6 Serve with creamed potatoes to soak up the creamy sauce.

Lancashire Pigeon Pie

✦ SERVES 4–6 ✦

*This is one of the most delicious dishes in the British repertoire, and has been
made in the old town of Bolton for generations.*

25g (1oz) butter	150ml (5fl oz) chicken stock
1 tablespoon cooking oil	2 tablespoons double cream
450g (1lb) pigeon meat	5 tablespoons Rowan Jelly (page 146)
225g (8oz) rump steak, thinly sliced	275g (10oz) Puff Pastry (page 153)
salt and freshly ground black pepper	2 tablespoons fresh parsley
6 slices rindless streaky bacon,	milk, for glazing
finely chopped	2 slices of white bread, cut into quarters
8 shallots, sliced	2 tablespoons olive oil
1 small carrot, diced	25g (1oz) butter
85ml (3fl oz) red wine	

1 Preheat the oven to 200°C/400°F/gas 6.

2 Melt the butter with the cooking oil in a large saucepan, add the pigeon meat and sliced
rump steak and cook for 3 minutes to seal the meat all over. Season with salt and pepper, add
the bacon, shallots and carrot, and cook for a further 3 minutes, stirring. Add the wine and
chicken stock, bring to the boil, and simmer for 25 minutes on a low heat, reducing the stock
by at least one-third.

3 Allow to cool slightly, then blend in the double cream and rowan jelly.

4 Roll out the pastry and use two-thirds of it to line a 1.1 litre (2 pint) pie dish. Place the meat
mixture into the pie dish and sprinkle with parsley. Roll out the remaining pastry to make a lid,
brush with a little milk, and bake in the centre of the preheated oven for 25 minutes.

5 Fry the bread in the hot oil and butter and serve round the pie.

Creamy Grouse Pie with Bacon and Shallots

✦ SERVES 4–6 ✦

In Scotland and Yorkshire grouse pie is always served with fried bread and rowan jelly.
In this version the rowan jelly is incorporated into the pie itself.

25g (1oz) butter	150ml (5fl oz) chicken stock
1 tablespoon cooking oil	2 tablespoons double cream
450g (1lb) grouse meat, chopped	5 tablespoons Rowan Jelly (page 146)
150g (5oz) duck livers, chopped	275g (10oz) Puff Pastry (page 153)
salt and freshly ground black pepper	2 tablespoons fresh parsley
6 slices rindless streaky bacon,	milk, for glazing
finely chopped	2 slices of white bread, cut into quarters
8 shallots, sliced	2 tablespoons olive oil
1 small carrot, diced	25g (1oz) butter
85ml (3fl oz) red wine	

1 Preheat the oven to 200°C/400°F/gas 6.

2 Melt the butter with the cooking oil in a large saucepan. Add the grouse meat and duck livers and brown. Season with salt and pepper. Add the bacon, shallots and carrot and cook, stirring, for a further 3 minutes. Add the wine and chicken stock and bring to the boil. Simmer for 25 minutes on a low heat, reducing the stock by at least one-third.

3 Allow the meat mixture to cool slightly, then blend in the cream and rowan jelly.

4 Roll out two-thirds of the pastry to fit a 1.1 litre (2 pint) pie dish. Put the meat mixture into the pie dish and sprinkle with parsley. Roll out the remaining pastry to make a lid, brush the top with a little milk, and bake in the centre of the preheated oven for 25 minutes.

5 Fry the bread in the hot oil and butter and serve around the pie.

Grouse in Port Pie

✦ SERVES 4–6 ✦

*I would like to dedicate this recipe to the late Francis Coulson and
Brian Sack of the Sharrow Bay Country House Hotel.*

25g (1oz) butter	150ml (5fl oz) chicken stock
1 tablespoon cooking oil	2 tablespoons double cream
450g (1lb) grouse meat	5 tablespoons Cranberry Sauce (page 145)
1 rabbit, boned and diced	275g (10oz) Cheese Scone Pastry
225g (8oz) guinea fowl breast, diced	(page 154)
salt and freshly ground black pepper	2 tablespoons chopped fresh parsley
6 slices rindless streaky bacon,	milk, for glazing
finely chopped	2 slices of white bread, cut into quarters
8 shallots, sliced	2 tablespoons olive oil
1 small carrot, diced	25g (1oz) butter
85ml (3fl oz) port	

1 Preheat the oven to 200°C/400°F/gas 6.

2 Melt the butter with the cooking oil in a large saucepan. Add the grouse, rabbit and guinea fowl meat and cook for 5 minutes to seal the meat all over. Season with salt and pepper, add the bacon, shallots and carrot, and cook for a further 3 minutes, stirring. Add the port and chicken stock, bring to the boil, and simmer for 25 minutes on a low heat, reducing the stock by at least one-third.

3 Allow the grouse and sauce to cool slightly and blend in the double cream and cranberry sauce.

4 Roll out two-thirds of the pastry to fit a 1.1 litre (2 pint) pie dish. Put the meat mixture into the pie dish and sprinkle with chopped parsley. Roll out the remaining pastry to make a lid, brush the top with a little milk, and bake in the centre of the preheated oven for 25 minutes.

5 Fry the bread in the hot oil and butter and serve with the pie.

Roast Guinea Fowl and Cranberry Pie

✦ **SERVES 6** ✦

Guinea fowl is quite a mild tasting game bird, and the cranberries bring out the flavour.
It is good served either hot or cold.

50g (2oz) butter	**450g (1lb) roast guinea fowl meat, diced**
2 leeks, very finely sliced	**150g (5oz) Cranberry Sauce (page 145)**
8 shallots, sliced	**salt and freshly ground black pepper**
100g (4oz) button mushrooms	**175g (6oz) Shortcrust Pastry (page 152)**
25g (1oz) plain flour	**100g (4oz) Puff Pastry (page 153)**
300ml (10fl oz) fresh milk, warmed	**1 egg, beaten**
150ml (5fl oz) double cream	

1 Preheat the oven to 200°C/400°F/gas 6.

2 Melt the butter in a large saucepan and gently fry the leeks, shallots and mushrooms for about 10 minutes, stirring occasionally. Add the flour and cook for a further 2 minutes, then gradually add the warm milk and cream, stirring continuously until the sauce becomes thick and creamy.

3 Add the guinea fowl and cranberry sauce to the sauce, season well with salt and freshly ground black pepper, and leave to cool.

4 Roll out the shortcrust pastry and use to line a greased ovenproof pie dish. Pour in the cooled guinea fowl mixture, top with a puff pastry lid, brush with beaten egg, and bake in the centre of the preheated oven for 30 minutes.

Rabbit and Ham Pie

✦ SERVES **4** ✦

A traditional recipe using country ingredients.

450g (1lb) boneless rabbit, diced	a generous pinch of rosemary
225g (8oz) York ham, diced	a generous pinch of thyme
1 carrot, finely diced	300ml (10fl oz) chicken stock
350g (12oz) sliced potatoes	150ml (5fl oz) strong dry cider
1 large apple, peeled, cored and diced	1 large tablespoon cornflour, blended
12 button onions, peeled	with a little cider or water
100g (4oz) button mushrooms	350g (12oz) Shortcrust Pastry (page 152)
salt and freshly ground black pepper	1 egg, beaten
1 tablespoon chopped fresh parsley	

1 Preheat the oven to 220°C/425°F/gas 7.

2 Fill a 1.7 litre (3 pint) casserole dish with alternate layers of rabbit, ham, carrot, potato, apple, onions and mushrooms, seasoning each layer with salt, freshly ground black pepper and herbs.

3 Pour the stock and cider into the casserole, cover and bake in the centre of the oven for about 30 minutes. Thicken the stock with the cornflour paste.

4 Roll out the pastry and make a lid to fit the casserole. Trim the edge, sealing the pie all round, and make a small hole in the centre of the pastry to allow the steam to come through. Brush with egg, and bake in the centre of the preheated oven for 1 hour at 180°C/350°F/gas 4.

Cold Rabbit Pie with Apple, Almonds and Port

✦ SERVES 6 ✦

*The original of this recipe is a wonderful hot pie from the Basque country. For a variation
in flavour try using pears instead of apples and add a little Calvados.*

900g (2lb) rabbit meat, chopped	1 quantity Hot Water Pastry (page 152)
50g (2oz) onion, finely chopped	1 egg, beaten
150ml (¼ pint) port	300ml (½ pint) aspic jelly, made up from
2 tablespoons brandy	a packet with wine and stock
½ teaspoon dried sage	
1 tablespoon Dijon mustard	FOR THE STUFFING
1 Bramley apple, peeled and coarsely grated	85g (3oz) breadcrumbs
2 tablespoons blanched almonds, roughly chopped	1 teaspoon dried basil
salt and freshly ground black pepper	50g (2oz) minced onion
	50g (2oz) minced Bramley apple
	150ml (5fl oz) beef stock
	225g (8oz) skinned black pudding, mashed

1 Preheat the oven to 200°C/400°F/gas 6.

2 Mix the rabbit with the onion, port, brandy, sage, mustard, apple and almonds and season well.

3 Mix all the stuffing ingredients together.

4 Line the bottom of a pie mould with two-thirds of the hot water pastry, putting it around the base and sides. Quarter fill the lined tin with meat mixture. Put a layer of stuffing mixture on top, and repeat the layers until you have three of meat and two of stuffing.

5 Roll out the remaining pastry and make a lid to fit the pie. Make a hole in the centre of the pie lid. Decorate with pastry leaves, paint with egg glaze and bake in the preheated oven for 35 minutes. Reduce to 180°C/350°F/gas 4 and bake for a further hour.

6 Remove the pie from the oven and allow it to cool. When cold, pour in some aspic jelly, made up with a little wine and stock. When the aspic has set, wrap the pie in clingfilm and leave to mature for 2 days.

Devonshire Hare Pie

✦ Serves 4 ✦

This pie is disappearing from today's menus and it really is a loss. The flavour and texture of hare meat is something that you cannot describe until you have actually eaten it. I think Beatrix Potter has a lot to answer for! You cannot successfully substitute any meat other than rabbit for this recipe.

350g (12oz) Shortcrust Pastry (page 152)	1 tablespoon freshly chopped parsley
450g (1lb) boneless hare meat, diced	a generous pinch of rosemary
100g (4oz) York ham, diced	a generous pinch of thyme
1 carrot, finely diced	150ml (5fl oz) strong dry cider
350g (12oz) potatoes, sliced	150ml (5fl oz) Game Stock (page 141)
1 large apple, peeled, cored and diced	150ml (5fl oz) Sauce Poivrade (page 145)
12 button onions	15g (½oz) butter, softened
100g (4oz) button mushrooms	15g (½oz) flour
salt and freshly ground black pepper	1 egg, beaten

1 Preheat the oven to 220°C/425°F gas 7.

2 Fill a 1.7 litre (3 pint) casserole dish with alternate layers of hare, ham, carrots, potatoes, onions and mushrooms, seasoning each layer with salt, pepper and herbs.

3 Pour in the cider, stock and Sauce Poivrade, then cover the casserole and bake in the centre of the preheated oven for about 45 minutes. Stir in a *beurre manié*, made by blending together the softened butter and flour. Reduce the oven temperature to 180°C/350°F/gas 4.

4 Roll out the pastry to make a lid and place on top of the casserole. Trim the edges, seal the pie all round, and make a small hole in the centre of the pastry to allow the steam to come through. Brush with egg and bake in the centre of the oven for 1 hour.

My Hunting Herb Pie

✦ **SERVES 4** ✦

I created this pie with Melton Mowbray in mind, a version of the famous pork pie.

1 quantity Hot Water Pastry (page 152)	**1 sprig of fresh marjoram**
1 egg, beaten	**1 sprig of fresh mint**
150ml (5fl oz) aspic jelly made up	**salt**
from a packet	**6 peppercorns**

FOR THE PORK STOCK	**FOR THE PIE FILLING**
450g (1lb) pork bones	**450g (1lb) mixed game meat**
1 pig's foot	**450g (1lb) Eldon Blue pork, cut into**
600ml (1 pint) water	**5mm (¼ inch) dice**
1 large onion, chopped	**generous pinch of salt**
1 carrot, chopped	**generous pinch of freshly ground**
1 bay leaf	**white pepper**
2 sage leaves	**1 teaspoon anchovy essence**
1 sprig of fresh thyme	

1 Put all the stock ingredients into a large pan and bring to the boil. Simmer for 2 hours or more, until the stock has reduced to 300ml (½ pint). Check the seasoning and allow the stock to cool, then skim off the fat. Pour the stock through a fine non-metallic sieve and set aside until needed.

2 Combine all the filling ingredients in a bowl, adding 2 tablespoons of the pork stock.

3 Make the hot water pastry and use to line a pork pie tin, loaf tin or cake tin with removable base, leaving enough pastry to make a lid.

4 Place the pie case on to a baking tray and put in the filling. Roll out the remaining pastry to make a lid and put it on, crimping the edges carefully. Make a hole in the centre of the lid to allow the steam out during the cooking process.

5 Preheat the oven to 200°C/400°F/gas 6 and bake in the lower part of the oven for 2 hours.

6 Ten minutes before the cooking time is up, remove the pie from the oven and brush with egg. Return to the oven for the final 10 minutes. Turn the oven off without opening, and leave the pie for 1 hour.

7 Reheat the aspic jelly until just warm. Stir into the stock and pour into the hole in the top of the pie.

8 Let the pie cool then wrap in clingfilm and refrigerate for at least 1 day. Serve, garnished with fresh herbs.

My Favourite Venison and Chestnut Pie

✦ SERVES 4 ✦

Go to town on the decoration of this pie and it will make a wonderful dish for a celebration.

900g (2lb) minced venison	**FOR THE STUFFING**
50g (2oz) finely chopped onion	50g (2oz) white breadcrumbs
150ml (¼ pint) dry white wine	50g (2oz) minced onion
2 tablespoons brandy	75g (3oz) chestnuts, chopped
½ teaspoon dried sage	50g (2oz) minced Bramley apple
1 tablespoon Dijon mustard	1 tablespoon chopped sage
1 Bramley apple, peeled and coarsely grated	225g (8oz) black pudding, skin removed, finely chopped
salt and freshly ground black pepper	a little stock
1 quantity Hot Water Pastry (page 152)	
1 egg, beaten	
120ml (3½fl oz) aspic jelly made up from a packet with a little wine and stock	

1 Preheat the oven to 200°C/400°F/gas 6.

2 Mix the minced venison with the onion, wine, brandy, sage, mustard, apple and seasoning.

3 In a separate bowl mix all the stuffing ingredients, adding enough hot stock to bind the mixture.

4 Line the bottom of a pie mould with two-thirds of the pastry. Quarter-fill the lined tin with the meat mixture and put a layer of stuffing mixture on top. Repeat the layers until you have 3 of venison and 2 of stuffing.

5 Roll out the remaining pastry, and make a lid for the pie. Make a hole in the centre. Decorate the pie with pastry leaves, brush with beaten egg, and bake in the preheated oven for 35 minutes. Reduce the oven to 180°C/350°F/gas 4 and bake for a further hour.

6 Remove the pie from the oven and allow it to cool. When cool, pour in some aspic jelly, made up with a little wine and stock.

7 When the aspic has set, wrap the pie in clingfilm and allow it to mature for 2 days.

Onion and Game Tart

✦ **SERVES 4** ✦

This is based on a traditional French recipe I tasted in Brittany. You can use any cooked game.

250g (8oz) Shortcrust Pastry (page 152)	**225g (8oz) cooked game meat, thinly sliced**
125g (4oz) butter	**284ml (10fl oz) single cream**
2 garlic cloves, crushed	**4 eggs, beaten**
1kg (2lb) onions	**salt and freshly ground black pepper**
1 teaspoon ground coriander	

1 Preheat the oven to 200°C/400°F/gas 6.

2 Roll out the pastry on a floured board and line a 20cm (8 inch) flan dish. Cover this with foil and bake blind for 20 minutes. Remove the foil, brush the pastry with beaten egg and return to the oven for 5 minutes. Lower the oven temperature to 170°C/325°F/gas 3.

3 Melt the butter in a large saucepan. Add the garlic and onions and cook for 10 minutes, then stir in the coriander and cook for a further 4 minutes.

4 Spread the mixture over the pastry and arrange the sliced game meat on top. Blend the cream and eggs together, season this well with salt and freshly ground black pepper, then pour the mixture over the onions and game.

5 Return to the oven and cook for 35–40 minutes, until the filling sets.

6 Garnish with fresh parsley and tarragon leaves, and serve with a glass of ice-cold cider.

TERRINES AND PATES

The difference between a pâté and a terrine used to be defined by the fact that a pâté was baked in pastry. Over the years these definitions have changed, and now there is little difference between them. Both are cooked in the oven in a terrine mould or bread tin, and can either be unmoulded on to a plate or not, depending on how firm the mixture is. Rillettes and other potted meats are usually served from the dish in which they were cooked. They are made by baking the meat with seasoning in a pottery dish until the meat falls apart, so that it can be shredded with forks and mixed with the fat it has rendered.

Game meat and fish make delicious pâtés and terrines, and you will find a varied selection in this chapter. Some are smooth and some are more chunky. Flavourings are important: juniper berries, mushrooms and spices give individual characteristics.

Smooth Duck and Pigeon Pâté

✦ SERVES 4 ✦

The addition of black pudding makes this recipe more interesting.

225g (8oz) breast of pigeon, sliced	2 teaspoons grated orange rind
225g (8oz) duck livers, minced	½ teaspoon mace
225g (8oz) duck breast, sliced	4 tablespoons orange curaçao
225g (8oz) black pudding, cubed	3 tablespoons brandy
1 onion, finely chopped	salt and freshly ground black pepper
1 teaspoon crushed garlic	2 eggs
4 juniper berries, crushed	285g (10oz) rindless smoked streaky bacon

1 Place all the ingredients except the bacon into a food mixer and blend them thoroughly.

2 Line a 1 litre (1¾ pint) terrine with streaky bacon, letting the rashers hang over the edge. Pour in the meat mixture and fold over the bacon to cover.

3 Cover the terrine with foil and leave to mature for 4 hours.

4 Preheat the oven to 170°C/325°F/gas 3. Place the terrine in a bain-marie or a deep tray half-filled with water and cook for 90 minutes. After cooling, leave to mature for at least 2 days before serving.

Olde English Game Terrine

✦ SERVES 4 ✦

Use breast meat from your favourite game birds for this recipe – I usually use quail, pheasant and grouse.
You can use ordinary pork instead of Eldon Blue, but the flavour will not be the same.

450g (1lb) breast of game (quail, pheasant, grouse etc)	285g (10oz) minced venison
2 tablespoons brandy	1 egg, beaten with 1 tablespoon cream
4 tablespoons port	4 shallots, minced
200g (8oz) pork fat, finely chopped	4 tablespoons Madeira
285g (10oz) minced Eldon Blue pork (page 91)	salt and freshly ground black pepper
	6 juniper berries, crushed
	225g (8oz) rindless smoked streaky bacon

1 If using quail and pheasant breast, cut into strips and marinate in the brandy and port for 2 hours. Finely chop grouse, if using.

2 Thoroughly blend all the rest of the ingredients except the streaky bacon in a large bowl. Stir in the chopped grouse. Chill for 2 hours while the quail and pheasant breasts are marinating.

3 Meanwhile line a 1 litre (1¾ pint) terrine with the streaky bacon, ensuring that enough hangs over the edge to fold back and cover the pâté. Put half the minced mixture into the terrine and lay the strips of quail and pheasant on top. Finish with the rest of the mixture.

4 Cover the terrine with the overhanging streaky bacon, lay a piece of buttered foil over the top, and put a lid on the terrine.

5 Preheat the oven to 170°C/325°F/gas 3. Put the terrine in a large baking tray half-filled with water and bake in the centre of the preheated oven for 2 hours, adding more water when necessary.

6 Allow to cool naturally and then chill for 4 hours before serving.

Julian Groom's Potted Game

✦ SERVES 4 ✦

I have numerous recipes for potted game, but this is the simplest and easiest, given to me by a dear friend of mine who is general manager of Le Meridian, Poona, India.

100g (4oz) butter	2 tablespoons Rowan Jelly (page 146)
450g (1lb) cooked game, minced	225g (8oz) cooked venison, roughly sliced
100g (4oz) cooked duck livers, minced	8 orange slices
1 teaspoon grated fresh ginger	10 black olives, stoned
freshly ground black pepper	100g (4oz) smoked duck breast

1 Put the butter, minced game, duck livers, ginger, freshly ground black pepper and rowan jelly into a bowl and mix thoroughly. Layer the minced mixture with the slices of cooked venison in small individual buttered pots or one large earthenware dish. Top with orange slices and olives.

2 Cut the smoked duck breast into small diamond shapes and use to garnish the edge of the pots or dish.

3 Chill for 4 hours and serve with home-made bread.

Terrine of Wild Rabbit

✦ SERVES 6–8 ✦

Quail meat gives this terrine extra flavour and colour.

450g (1lb) rabbit meat, cut into small pieces	1 red pepper, diced
250g (½lb) hare meat, cut into small pieces	1 yellow pepper, diced
250g (½lb) pork fillet, diced	a pinch of mace
225g (8oz) quail meat, diced	a pinch of nutmeg
125g (4oz) butter, melted	a pinch of crushed cloves
1 green pepper, diced	salt and freshly ground black pepper
	Clarified Butter (page 151)

1 Preheat the oven to 180°C/350°F/gas 4.

2 Place all the ingredients except the clarified butter into a large saucepan and bring them gradually to the boil. Simmer for 30 minutes, then transfer the mixture into a 900g (2lb) terrine. Cover with cooking foil and place in a bain-marie or baking tray, with hot water to come half-way up the sides of the terrine. Cook in the centre of the oven for 60 minutes.

3 When the terrine is cooked, allow it to cool and then cover the top with clarified butter. Chill in the refrigerator for at least 3–4 hours before serving.

Terrine of Woodcock

✦ Serves 4–6 ✦

Serve this with brioche or melba toast, with a little cranberry sauce, if you like.

450g (1lb) woodcock meat, diced	1 yellow pepper, diced
250g (½lb) ham, diced	a pinch of mace
100g (4oz) duck livers, finely chopped	a pinch of nutmeg
100g (4oz) butter	6 tablespoons port
2 apples, peeled, cored and diced	salt and freshly ground black pepper
1 green pepper, diced	Clarified Butter (page 151)

1 Preheat the oven to 180°C/350°F/gas 4.

2 Put all the ingredients except the clarified butter into a large saucepan and bring them gradually to the boil. Let the saucepan simmer for 30 minutes, stirring every 3 minutes or so.

3 Put the mixture into a 1 litre (1¾ pint) terrine, cover with cooking foil, and stand in a bain-marie or baking tray. Pour in hot water to come half-way up the sides of the terrine. Cook in the centre of the oven for 60 minutes.

4 Allow the terrine to cool, then cover with clarified butter and chill in the refrigerator for at least 3–4 hours before serving.

Terrine of Hare and Ham with a Rich Cranberry and Shallot Marmalade

✦ SERVES 4 ✦

One of my golden oldies from yesteryear. The black pudding must not be too fatty.

450g (1lb) boneless hare meat, chopped	3 eggs, beaten
100ml (4fl oz) brandy	450g (1lb) lean York ham, diced
225g (8oz) minced pork	450g (1lb) rindless streaky bacon
225g (8oz) black pudding, diced	25g (1oz) butter
3 large onions, chopped	4 tablespoons cranberries
grated rind of 1 orange	1 tablespoon brown sugar
salt and freshly ground black pepper	8 shallots, chopped
	orange slices to garnish

1 Preheat the oven to 180°C/350°F/gas 4.

2 Remove any fat or sinews from the hare meat and put it into a bowl with the brandy. Leave to marinate for 3 hours.

3 Add the pork and black pudding to the hare meat, with 3 tablespoons of chopped onion, the orange rind, seasoning and eggs. Blend the mixture thoroughly. Stir the pieces of ham into the mixture. Line a 1.4 litre (2½ pint) ovenproof terrine with slices of streaky bacon. Put in the hare mixture, cover with the rest of the bacon, then put greased foil over the top.

4 Stand the terrine in a baking tin and add hot water to come half-way up the sides. Bake in the centre of the preheated oven for 90 minutes. Remove the foil and allow to cool naturally, then chill for at least 4 hours before serving.

5 Fry the remaining onions gently for 2 minutes in the butter. Add the cranberries, brown sugar and shallots and cook for 5 minutes more. Pour a little of the cranberry and shallot marmalade on to individual plates and serve with a generous slice of the terrine, garnished with slices of orange, and fresh bread.

Hart of England Smooth Venison Pâté

✦ SERVES 4 ✦

For a smooth venison and cranberry pâté, simply add to the ingredients 170g (6oz) of cooked cranberries with 1 tablespoon of honey. You can substitute your favourite rum or whisky for the brandy to make a festive pâté, and you can also replace the venison with other game – but use only the breast meat or other quality cut.

100g (4oz) pork fat, finely diced	½ teaspoon allspice
225g (8oz) lean pork, minced	½ teaspoon mace
225g (8oz) lean venison, minced	4 tablespoons red wine
225g (8oz) venison livers, minced	3 tablespoons brandy
1 onion, finely chopped	salt and freshly ground black pepper
1 teaspoon crushed garlic	2 eggs
10 juniper berries, crushed	285g (10 oz) rindless smoked streaky bacon

1 Put all the ingredients except the bacon into a food mixer and blend them thoroughly.

2 Line a 1 litre (1¾ pint) terrine with the bacon, letting the rashers hang over the edge. Pour in the meat mixture and fold over the bacon to cover. Cover the terrine with foil and leave to mature for 6 hours.

3 Preheat the oven to 170°C/325°F/gas 3.

4 Stand the terrine in a bain-marie or a deep tray half-filled with water, and cook for 2 hours. After cooling, leave to mature for at least 2 days before serving.

Rillettes of Eldon Blue Pork

✦ SERVES 10–12 ✦

This really is the business, and twins a special French recipe with my favourite Eldon Blue Pork.
It should be served with fresh crusty French bread and a bottle of cold Chardonnay.
Save the pork fat for sealing and frying your game recipes.

900g (2lb) Eldon Blue Pork belly, cut into fine strips	1 sprig of parsley
340g (12oz) pork fat, finely diced	1 sprig of rosemary
salt and freshly ground black pepper	190ml (7fl oz) chicken stock
celery salt	Clarified Butter (page 151)
3 garlic cloves, crushed with a little olive oil	

1 Preheat the oven to 150°C/300°F/gas 2.

2 Lay the strips of pork and pork fat on a large board and season well with salt and pepper and celery salt.

3 Put the garlic into the base of a 1.4 litre (2½ pint) terrine, packing the meat and fat in tightly. Push the herbs into the centre of the meat and pour over just enough chicken stock to cover. Cover with a lid or foil and bake in the centre of the preheated oven for 5 hours, stirring every hour.

4 Place a sieve over a bowl. Remove the terrine from the oven and turn the contents into the sieve. Remove the herbs and either shred the pork with two forks to make a coarse pâté, or put it through a blender for 6 seconds to make a smoother pâté. Taste and adjust the seasoning. Pack the meat back into the terrine and let it stand for 1 hour. Pour over just enough clarified butter to cover and refrigerate for 1 day, allowing the butter to set. The rillettes will keep for at least 8 weeks in the refrigerator if covered properly.

Individual Terrines of Wild Scottish Salmon

✦ **SERVES 4–6** ✦

Wild salmon is expensive, but you can sometimes get cheaper ends of wild salmon from your fishmonger.

450g (1lb) wild salmon ends	2 tablespoons port
a pinch of nutmeg	2 tablespoons double cream
a pinch of mace	1 lemon, thinly sliced
100g (4oz) butter, softened	sprigs of parsley
salt and freshly ground black pepper	

1 Preheat the oven to 180°C/350°F/gas 4.

2 Place the chopped wild salmon ends into a large bowl with the nutmeg, mace, butter, seasoning, port and cream. Blend until very smooth.

3 Place the salmon mixture into individual earthenware terrines. Stand them in a bain-marie or a deep tray, with a little hot water to come half-way up the sides of the terrines. Cover with buttered greaseproof paper and weight them down. Cook in the centre of the preheated oven for 45 minutes. Allow to cool naturally then refrigerate for 4 hours.

4 Remove the greaseproof paper and decorate with slices of fresh lemon and sprigs of parsley. Serve with warm toast and butter.

Smoked Wild Trout and Beetroot Pâté

✦ **SERVES 4** ✦

One of those starters that you could also serve as a main course, with toast and a glass of ice-cold Chardonnay.

450g (1lb) smoked wild trout, bones and skin removed	2 tablespoons brandy
zest and juice of 1 lime	1 tablespoon aspic jelly (made up from a packet)
175g (6oz) long-life beetroot, puréed	4 tablespoons double cream
175g (6oz) cream cheese	salt and freshly ground black pepper
1 tablespoon capers, finely chopped	Clarified Butter (page 151)
1 tablespoon chives, finely chopped	

1 Flake the fish into a large mixing bowl. Add all the other ingredients except the clarified butter one at a time, and blend to a smooth paste.

2 Transfer the pâté into a serving dish and pour over clarified butter to cover the top. Garnish with lime zest and fresh parsley and chill for 3 hours or until required. Serve with melba toast.

BASICS AND ACCOMPANIMENTS

In this chapter you will find recipes for all the traditional accompaniments to game, such as sauces, relishes, game chips and fried breadcrumbs. Also given here are recipes for those standards that are always needed, such as stocks, pastries and marinades.

Sauces are a particular interest of mine, as they are of most chefs. The ones given here may seem time-consuming, but I can assure you that the results are worth it.

MARINADES

Tom's Marinade for Game

Use this marinade for any kind of game.

1 bottle of red wine	50g (2oz) parsley stalks
250ml (½ pint) cider	salt
125ml (¼ pint) vegetable oil	1 tablespoon black peppercorns
200g (8oz) onions, sliced	1 sprig of thyme
200g (8oz) carrots, sliced	2 bay leaves
100g (4oz) celery, chopped	4 tablespoons garlic vinegar

1 Mix all the ingredients together in a large glass or earthenware bowl.

2 Add the game and leave to marinate for 12 hours at least, turning occasionally. For perfect results leave it for 24–48 hours.

European Game Marinade

After researching marinades from all over Europe, I have combined many flavours to make this perfect game marinade. It can be used for any game and is ideal for food that is to be barbecued.

150ml (5fl oz) Giblet Stock (page 142)	1 teaspoon grated fresh ginger
150ml (5fl oz) red wine	1 teaspoon coriander seeds, crushed
3 tablespoons honey	1 teaspoon lemon juice
2 tablespoons tomato ketchup	6 black peppercorns
2 tablespoons olive oil	1 teaspoon fennel seeds, crushed
2 tablespoons truffle oil	4 bay leaves
2 tablespoons light soy sauce	a pinch of chilli powder
2 tablespoons Worcestershire sauce	a pinch of salt
2 garlic cloves, crushed	

1 Put all the ingredients in a large glass or earthenware bowl. Add the game and leave to marinate for 12 hours, turning occasionally.

White Wine, Honey and Garlic Marinade

This recipe is a typical American marinade for use with feathered game and fish.

300ml (10fl oz) good white wine	2 bay leaves
150ml (5fl oz) clear honey	1 teaspoon coriander seeds, crushed
150ml (5fl oz) olive oil	2 tablespoons chopped fresh parsley
4 garlic cloves, crushed	1 teaspoon fresh thyme
1 teaspoon fennel seeds, crushed	

1 Put all the ingredients in a large glass or earthenware bowl. Add the game and marinate for 4 hours. Use the marinade to baste the game during cooking.

STOCKS AND FISH COURT-BOUILLON

Whatever soup or sauce you are making, it will taste better if you use a home-made stock. Make use of scraps of game, meat, poultry carcasses, bones and vegetable trimmings that would otherwise be thrown away, but do not use the skin from game because it is far too pungent and fatty.

Today many people use stock cubes – I do not use these myself, but appreciate that they save time, so please use them if you like. Most stocks need to simmer for at least 3 hours to produce the best flavour, while a stock cube needs only a few minutes, and can be improved with the addition of game, fish or vegetables.

When making soups or sauces, always use a large heavy-based saucepan with a well-fitting lid, and, should you be able to afford it, a copper saucepan is far better than any other saucepan. To remove all fat from a soup or sauce, reduce the heat completely and sprinkle a few drops of cold water over the sauce. This will cause the fat to rise, so that it can be easily removed.

Game Stock

My basic recipe, which I use again and again.

450g (1lb) game bones	2 large carrots, sliced
450g (1lb) shin of venison	2 bouquets garni
450g (1lb) mixed game meat	4 white peppercorns
50g (2oz) dripping	8 juniper berries
2 leeks, sliced	4 tablespoons white wine vinegar
1 large onion, sliced	1 sprig of thyme
1 celery stick, sliced	salt and freshly ground black pepper

1 Preheat the oven to 220°C/425°F/gas 7. Blanch the bones for 10 minutes in boiling water, then put them with the chopped meat and the dripping in a large roasting tin. Brown the bones in the centre of the preheated oven for 40 minutes.

2 Remove the bones to a large deep flameproof casserole or pan, and add the vegetables and all the other ingredients. Cover with water and bring the contents slowly to the boil. Remove any scum from the surface and cover the casserole or pan with a tight-fitting lid. Simmer the stock over the lowest possible heat for 3 hours, to extract all the flavour from the bones and vegetables. Top up with hot water if necessary.

3 Strain the stock through a fine sieve into a large bowl. Leave the stock to settle for 5 minutes, then remove the fat from the surface by drawing absorbent kitchen paper across the top. Correct the seasoning and it is ready to use.

Giblet Stock

Another basic stock recipe, this time making use of giblets.

50g (2oz) duck fat	**4 white peppercorns**
450g (1lb) mixed turkey, duck and grouse giblets	**8 juniper berries**
2 leeks, sliced	**4 tablespoons white wine vinegar**
1 large onion, sliced	**1 litre (1¾ pints) Game Stock (page 141) or water**
1 celery stick, sliced	**1 sprig of thyme**
2 large carrots, sliced	**salt and freshly ground black pepper**
2 bouquets garni	

1 Heat the duck fat in a large saucepan. Chop the giblets and add them to the pan with the leeks, onion, celery and carrots. Cook for 10 minutes, then add the rest of the ingredients and bring the contents slowly to the boil. Remove any scum from the surface and cover the saucepan with a tight-fitting lid. Simmer the stock over a low heat for 1½ hours to extract all the flavour from the giblets and vegetables. Top up with hot water if necessary.

2 Strain the stock through a fine sieve into a large bowl. Leave to settle for 5 minutes, then remove the fat from the surface by drawing absorbent kitchen paper across the top. Correct the seasoning and it is ready to use.

Fish Court-Bouillon

Many fish recipes require court-bouillon, a flavoured liquid in which the fish can be poached gently. It is always handy to have some in the fridge, so I am including a recipe here.

50g (2oz) butter	**900g (2lb) fish trimmings (cod, salmon, haddock, etc.)**
2 tablespoons olive oil	
1 carrot, finely chopped	**juice and zest of 1 lemon**
8 shallots, finely chopped	**1 bouquet garni**
1 celery stick, finely chopped	**1 bay leaf**
425ml (15fl oz) water	**salt and freshly ground black pepper**
425ml (15fl oz) dry white wine	

1 Heat the butter and olive oil in a large saucepan and cook the vegetables gently for about 5 minutes until the onion becomes transparent. Add the rest of the ingredients and bring to the boil, then cover the pan and simmer for 45 minutes.

2 Pour the court-bouillon into a lidded container and refrigerate until required. It will keep for 5 days, covered, in the refrigerator.

SAUCES AND ACCOMPANIMENTS

Espagnole Sauce

*This is one of the classic French sauces, and very important to both English and French chefs.
It takes a long time to make, but the result is worth it.*

25g (1oz) butter	100g (4oz) carrot, finely diced
25g (1oz) flour	100g (4oz) onion, finely diced
1 tablespoon tomato purée	50g (2oz) celery, finely diced
1 litre (1¾ pints) beef stock	50g (2oz) leeks, finely diced
2 tablespoons wine vinegar	50g (2oz) fennel, finely diced
a little oil or butter	a sprig of thyme
100g (4oz) rindless smoked bacon, finely diced	1 small bay leaf
	salt and freshly ground black pepper

1 Heat the butter in a heavy-based saucepan and stir in the flour to make a roux. Do not let the mixture burn. Add the tomato purée to the roux, then slowly add the hot stock and the vinegar.

2 In a separate saucepan heat the oil or butter and cook the bacon and vegetables until light golden. Drain the vegetables, add them to the sauce with the herbs and seasoning, and simmer slowly for at least 4 hours.

3 Skim with a ladle, strain through a fine sieve into a clean pan, and reheat when needed.

Demi-glace Sauce

*Professional kitchens are never without a supply of demi-glace; it is such an important
sauce for anyone who takes their cooking seriously. It is the base for all dark sauces,
and it is used in many of the sauces to be served with game.*

1 litre (1¾ pints) Espagnole Sauce, see above	1 litre (1¾ pints) beef stock
	salt and freshly ground black pepper

1 Put the Espagnole sauce and stock in a large heavy-bottomed saucepan, bring to the boil, and simmer until reduced by half. Skim the surface well, then pass the sauce through a fine non-metallic sieve. Taste and adjust the seasoning.

2 The sauce is now ready to use, or it can be left to cool and then refrigerated for up to 5 days.

Bordelaise Sauce

Diced poached beef marrow is the classic ingredient in this sauce, which is often served with grilled meats.

150ml (5fl oz) claret	salt and freshly ground black pepper
2 tablespoons red wine vinegar	300ml (10fl oz) Demi-glace Sauce
50g (2oz) shallots or onions, chopped	(page 143)
1 bay leaf	75g (3oz) beef marrow, diced
1 sprig of thyme	

1 Put the claret, vinegar, shallots, herbs, salt and pepper into a small saucepan over a high heat, and boil until reduced by at least a quarter. Add the demi-glace, lower the heat, and simmer for at least 20 minutes. Taste and adjust the seasoning, then pass the sauce through a fine non-metallic sieve. Stir in the beef marrow.

Sauce Chasseur

A classic sauce for game.

25g (1oz) butter or margarine	100g (4oz) tomatoes, skinned and chopped
25g (1oz) shallots or onions, chopped	250ml (½ pint) Demi-glace Sauce (page 143)
1 small garlic clove, crushed	a pinch of finely chopped fresh parsley
50g (2oz) button mushrooms, sliced	a pinch of finely chopped fresh tarragon
4 tablespoons dry white wine	salt and freshly ground black pepper
4 tablespoons white wine vinegar	

1 Melt the butter in a small saucepan on a medium heat. Add the shallots or onions and cook gently for 2 minutes. Add the garlic and mushrooms and cook for a further 2 minutes.

2 Drain away the fat, add the wine and vinegar and simmer until reduced by half. Add the tomatoes and the demi-glace, and simmer for 8 minutes. Add the herbs and season.

3 For a fuller flavour, use red wine or port instead of white wine.

Sauce Poivrade

Another game classic.

25g (1oz) butter	6 juniper berries
50g (2oz) carrot	6 black peppercorns
50g (2oz) shallots	4 tablespoons tarragon vinegar
1 sprig of fresh parsley	250ml (½ pint) Demi-glace Sauce (page 143)
1 bay leaf	salt and freshly ground black pepper
a little thyme	

1 Heat the butter in a medium saucepan. Add all the vegetables and cook until brown. Drain away the fat and add the herbs, juniper berries, peppercorns and tarragon vinegar. Cook until the sauce has reduced by half, then add the demi-glace and simmer for 25 minutes. Season with salt and pepper.

Madeira Sauce

Simply add 3 tablespoons of Madeira to 250ml (½ pint) of Demi-glace sauce (page 143), stir in 25g (1oz) butter, and season with salt and freshly ground black pepper.

Home-made Cranberry Sauce

✦ MAKES 1.4KG (3LB) ✦

Fruits vary in pectin and acid content, but you can now buy sugar with pectin, which will ensure a perfect set for your sauce. You can replace the cranberries in the recipe with your favourite fruit, using the same method.

1.4kg (3lb) cranberries	juice and zest of ½ lemon
900g (2lb) sugar with pectin	

1 Remove the stalks from the cranberries and wash and drain them well. Put them into a large bowl in layers with the sugar, and leave for 1 hour.

2 Put the cranberries into a large saucepan, add the lemon juice and zest and stir for 2 minutes. Bring to the boil. Boil rapidly for 5 minutes, then simmer for 10 minutes. Allow to cool for 15 minutes, removing any scum.

3 Stir the cranberries carefully and evenly through the sauce. Pot into warm jars, cover, label and date. This sauce will keep for up to 6 months.

Yorkshire Relish

This is one of the oldest preserves in Yorkshire history. In the inns and restaurants, if meat was covered with gravy the Yorkshireman became very suspicious, thinking it was yesterday's leftovers warmed up. So they would ask for game or meat with a sauceboat of Yorkshire relish.

600ml (1 pint) malt vinegar	1 tablespoon black treacle
100g (4oz) soft brown sugar	1 tablespoon Worcestershire sauce
1 teaspoon salt	1 tablespoon mushroom ketchup
6 black peppercorns	½ teaspoon freshly grated nutmeg
25g (1oz) chopped chillies	

1 Place all the ingredients into a saucepan and bring to the boil. Simmer for 10 minutes, then remove from the heat and allow the relish to cool.

2 Pour into warm sterilized bottles with cork or vinegar-proof tops. The relish will keep for about 18 months if stored in a dry, dark place, and will mature with age.

Rowan Jelly

A traditional accompaniment for game, excellent with any of the recipes in this book. The rowan berries must be just ripe and the apples sweet.

900g (2lb) rowan berries	2kg (4½lb) sugar with pectin
900g (2lb) Cox's Orange Pippins	

1 Remove any stalks from the rowan berries, wash and drain them. Peel, core and chop the apples.

2 Place the fruit into a large saucepan and just cover with water. Cook for 15 minutes, then strain the fruit and liquid through a fine sieve into a clean saucepan. Add the sugar. Boil rapidly for 15 minutes until the jelly is nearly at setting point, then pot and seal in warm sterilized jars.

Red Cabbage

Served with a game pie, this home-made red cabbage will become the talking point of the table. The cabbage you buy needs to be really firm for best results.

1 red cabbage	**50g (2oz) soft brown sugar**
100g (4oz) cooking salt	**600ml (1 pint) white wine vinegar**

1 Remove any discoloured leaves from the red cabbage. Cut the cabbage into quarters and cut out the stalk. Shred the cabbage finely. Place the shredded cabbage, salt and sugar in layers in a large basin. Cover with clingfilm and leave for 24 hours.

2 Rinse the cabbage in cold water, draining it well. Pack it quite loosely into jars, cover with white wine vinegar and seal.

3 Keep for at least 7 days before using, and use within 3 months or it will lose its crispness.

Traditional Bread Sauce

This sauce is excellent with roast game.

6 cloves	**225g (8oz) fresh white breadcrumbs**
1 medium onion	**salt and freshly ground black pepper**
425ml (15fl oz) milk	**2 tablespoons double cream**
a pinch of mace	**15g (½oz) butter**
4 peppercorns	

1 Stick the cloves into the onion and put this into a saucepan with the milk, mace and peppercorns. Bring to the boil, then remove the saucepan from the heat and leave to infuse, covered, for 35 minutes.

2 Strain the milk through a fine sieve into another clean saucepan and stir in the breadcrumbs. Return the saucepan to the heat, stirring continuously, until the mixture becomes quite thick.

3 Season the sauce well with salt and freshly ground black pepper, stir in the cream and butter, and serve warm.

Giblet Gravy

The perfect finish to a roast.

25g (1oz) butter	zest of 1 orange
285g (10oz) duck or grouse	zest of 1 lemon
giblets, chopped	2 tablespoons red wine vinegar
150ml (5fl oz) Madeira	1 teaspoon juniper berries
1 sprig of thyme	600ml (1 pint) Giblet Stock (page 142)
1 sprig of rosemary	salt and freshly ground black pepper

1 Heat the butter in a large saucepan and add the giblets. Cook for 10 minutes, then add the Madeira, thyme, rosemary, orange zest, lemon zest, vinegar and juniper berries. Cook for a further 5 minutes, then add the giblet stock. Bring to the boil, then simmer until reduced by one-third.

2 Strain through a fine sieve and season with salt and pepper.

Game Stuffing

*This is my mother's classic recipe for a traditional forcemeat, which can be used with any game.
For a more festive stuffing add 225g (8oz) chestnut purée, 3 tablespoons of dark rum and
1 teaspoon of freshly grated nutmeg to the ingredients below.*

225g (8oz) fresh white breadcrumbs	½ teaspoon chopped fresh thyme
225g (8oz) rindless streaky bacon	½ teaspoon chopped fresh sage
1 large onion, chopped	1 egg
100g (4oz) melted butter	juice of ½ lemon
100g (4oz) pork sausagemeat	1 teaspoon salt
2 tablespoons chopped fresh parsley	freshly ground black pepper

1 Put the breadcrumbs into a bowl. Chop the bacon into small pieces. Fry the bacon and onion for 4 minutes and add this to the bowl with the rest of the ingredients. Bind them all together to make a moist but not too wet stuffing.

Game Chips

Crisps are one of the best-selling food items around the world, and when they are made at home to serve with game they are known as game chips. The potatoes must be cut so thin that you can see through them – you can do this using a mandolin, the side of a cheese grater or a food processor.

450g (1lb) potatoes, peeled and very thinly sliced	peanut oil for deep-frying
	sea salt

1 Soak the thinly sliced potatoes in cold water for 40 minutes to remove excess starch. Dry them thoroughly in a clean tea towel, or on kitchen paper.

2 Heat the oil in a chip pan. Place half the potatoes into the frying basket, and when the oil is smoking carefully lower the potatoes into the hot oil and cook for 4–5 minutes until golden brown, shaking the basket every minute so that they do not stick together.

3 Drain them on kitchen paper, sprinkle them with salt, and put them under the grill for a few seconds to dry them out.

4 Repeat the process with the rest of the potatoes.

Potato Cakes

These are my choice for serving with guinea fowl

450g (1lb) cooked mashed potato	**salt and freshly ground black pepper**
25g (1oz) finely chopped onion	**plain flour**
1 egg, beaten with 2 tablespoons fresh milk	**50g (2oz) dripping**

1 Blend the potato, onion, egg, salt and pepper with just enough flour to stop the mixture becoming too moist. Shape into little flat cakes on a floured board.

2 Put the dripping into a frying pan and when it is hot add the potato cakes. Cook for 3 minutes on each side until they are golden brown.

Fried Breadcrumbs

Fried breadcrumbs are a traditional alternative to game chips for serving with game.
The breadcrumbs must be fresh – do not use packet breadcrumbs for this recipe.

50g (2oz) butter

1 teaspoon truffle oil (see below)

100g (4oz) fresh white breadcrumbs

1 Gently heat the butter and truffle oil in a frying pan. Add the breadcrumbs and fry them over a low heat, stirring all the time until the butter is absorbed by the breadcrumbs. Increase the heat and fry the breadcrumbs until they are evenly brown.

Truffle Oil

One of my favourite ingredients is L'Oro in Cucina, a dressing made from extra virgin olive oil with truffles, commonly known as truffle oil. It is one of my favourite products and is excellent for any cut of game. Simply pour a tablespoonful over your favourite cut of game before roasting. Truffle oil can be purchased by post from Gourmet World *(see Useful Addresses, page 155).*

Clarified Butter

A useful ingredient to have in the refrigerator, and essential for sealing pâtés and terrines.
225g (8oz) butter will produce 175g (6oz) of clarified butter.

1 Place the butter in a small saucepan and heat very gently, skimming off the foam as the butter heats up. The sediment will sink to the bottom of the pan.

2 When the butter is completely melted, remove the pan from the heat and leave it to stand for at least 4 minutes before straining it through a cheesecloth or fine muslin into a bowl.

3 Allow the clarified butter to cool a little before using.

PASTRY

Shortcrust Pastry

✦ MAKES 700G (1½LB) ✦

Good pastry should be light in texture. It is important to weigh the ingredients accurately and keep all the ingredients, utensils and your clean hands as cool as possible.

450g (1lb) plain flour	100g (4oz) butter
½ teaspoon salt	100g (4oz) lard

1 Sift the flour and salt into a clean bowl, then gently rub in the butter and lard until the mixture resembles fine breadcrumbs. Add enough cold water to make a stiff dough. Press the dough together with your fingertips. Sprinkle with a little sifted flour, then roll the pastry out on a lightly floured surface.

Hot Water Pastry

✦ MAKES ABOUT 900G (2LB) ✦

A traditional British pastry used for raised pies.

150g (5oz) lard	½ teaspoon salt
200ml (7fl oz) water	1 large egg yolk
350g (12oz) plain flour	

1 Put the lard and water into a saucepan and heat gently until the lard has melted. Bring the mixture slowly to the boil, remove from the heat, and beat in the flour and salt to form a soft dough.

2 Beat the egg yolk into the dough, cover with a damp cloth and leave to rest in a warm place for 15 minutes. Do not allow the dough to cool completely.

3 The pastry is now ready for use and must be used *immediately*.

Rosa Lewis's Suet Pastry

✦ MAKES ABOUT 900G (2LB) ✦

This is the pastry to use for Rosa's Quail Pudding (page 41).

450g (1lb) self-raising flour	pinch of mace
75g (3oz) butter, softened	pinch of powdered rosemary
140g (5oz) freshly shredded suet	1 medium egg
salt and freshly ground white pepper	1 tablespoon water

1 Put the flour, butter and suet into a bowl and season with a little salt, white pepper, mace and powdered rosemary. Rub together with your fingertips until the mixture resembles fine breadcrumbs.

2 Mix the egg and water, make a well in the centre of the flour mixture and pour in the egg. Mix together until a soft paste forms. Add a little more water if necessary. Turn the mixture out on to a floured work surface and knead to a soft but fairly firm dough. Leave to rest for 1 hour.

Puff Pastry

✦ MAKES 700G (1½LB) ✦

It is worth making a large batch of puff pastry and freezing half of it, because it is a time-consuming job. It will keep in the freezer for up to 3 months.

450g (1lb) plain flour	450g (1lb) butter
½ teaspoon salt	1 tablespoon lemon juice

1 Sift the flour and salt into a clean bowl. Gently rub in 100g (4oz) of the butter. Add the lemon juice and a little cold water to make a smooth dough.

2 Shape the remaining butter into a rectangle on a sheet of greaseproof paper.

3 Carefully roll out the dough on a lightly floured surface to a strip a little wider than the butter and twice the length. Place the butter on one half of the pastry and gently fold over the other half, pressing the edges with a floured rolling pin.

4 Leave the pastry in a cool place for 20 minutes to allow the butter to harden, then roll out on a lightly floured surface. Fold the bottom third up and the top third down, pressing the edges together with the rolling pin and turning the pastry so the folded edges are on the right and left of you. Roll and fold again, cover and leave in a cool place for 15 minutes. After this, repeat the process of rolling and folding 8 times. The pastry is now ready for use.

Cheese Scone Pastry

✦ **MAKES ABOUT 450G (1LB)** ✦

This is a very tasty original recipe from my mother's cookery book. It is ideal to use with any precooked game meat. Try breast of guinea fowl, pheasant or grouse wrapped in this very light pastry, or a mixture of vegetables and diced cooked game.

225g (8oz) self-raising flour, sifted	50g (2oz) Cheddar cheese, grated
50g (2oz) butter, softened	2 tablespoons shallots, finely chopped
50g (2oz) lard	6 tablespoons water, blended with
salt and freshly ground black pepper	50ml (2fl oz) yoghurt

1 Put the sifted flour, butter and lard into a bowl and season with a little salt and pepper. Rub together with your fingertips until the mixture resembles fine breadcrumbs.

2 Add the grated cheese and shallots and mix well in. Make a well in the centre of the flour and pour in the yoghurt mixture. Mix together to a soft paste. Turn the mixture out on to a floured work surface and knead to a soft but fairly firm dough.

APPENDIX

CIRCOTHERM TEMPERATURE CONVERSION CHART

The following conversion chart is for those of you who, like myself, use the excellent circotherm ovens.

COOKING GUIDE	CIRCOTHERM	CONVENTIONAL ELECTRIC		GAS MARK
	°C	°F	°C	
Braising	130	275	140	1
Casseroling	140	300	150	2
Steaming	150	325	170	3
Baking/Roasting	160	350-375	180-190	4-5
	170	400	200	6
Air Grilling	180	425	220	7

For more detailed instructions, please refer to your instruction manual

RECOMMENDED GAME SUPPLIERS

My thoughts here are on helping you to be able to purchase high quality Game products.

The Guild of Q Butchers is an amalgamation of the meat trades' three quality assurance schemes: 'Q' Guild Ltd., Shop with Assurance and Shop with Confidence. For a list of the Q Butchers in your area please write to: **Ross Muir Public Relations,** 7 Dunfermline Road, Limekilns, Fife KY11 3JU.

Fairfax Meadow are one of the UK's most innovative and respected catering butchers, serving the food service industry with a comprehensive range of products in the game, red and white meat sectors. Contact Fairfax Meadow on 0870 606 6066.

Aberdeen Foods Ltd
Unit 1
Broomiesburn Road
Ellon
Aberdeen AB41 9RD

Ashwood Agencies Ltd
Noel Stone
42 Drumalig Road
Carryduff
Belfast BT8 8EQ
01232 815117

Ashwood Fine Foods
Nick White
Unit 19, Preston Cold Store
Cromwell Road
Ribbleton
Preston PR2 6YD
01772 704849

Bain of Tarves
John Bain
Duthie Road
Tarves, Aberdeenshire
Scotland AB41 7JX
01651 852000

Christina Bookerville
Barrow Boar
Fosters Farm
South Barrow
Yeovil
Somerset BA22 7LN

Bourgoin UK
Cresswell House
Fieldway
Maes-y-Coed Rd
Heath
Cardiff CF1
01222 522525

John Bryan Organic Meats
8 The Wynd
Biggar
Scotland ML12 6BU
01899 221747

CDK Foods
Borrowdale House
49 Barkly Road
Leeds LS11 7EW
01532 711930

James Chapman
35 Glasgow Road
Wishaw ML2 7PG

Cherry Valley Farms
Rothwell
Lincolnshire LN7 6BR
01472 371271

Craig Farm Organic Meat
Dolau
Llandrindod Wells
Powys LD1 5TL
01597 951655

Jim Cruickshank
1 The Square
Fochabers
Morayshire

Eastbrook Farm (Organic Meats)
Bishopstone
Swindon
Wiltshire SN6 8PW
01793 790460

Fayre Game
Jeremy Blower
01744 616120

Fordhall Organic Farm
459 Halliwell Road
Bolton
Lancashire BL18 8DE

Fyne Game Of Inverary
Unit 3, Upper Riochan
Inverary
Argyll PA32 8UR
01499 2443-2055

The Ginger Pig
Harwell Manor
Harwell
Everton
Nottingham DN10 5BU
01777 816737

Green Label Poultry
Loomswood Farm
Debach
Woodbridge
Suffolk IP13 6JW
01473 735456

Hart of England Deer Farm
Mike Robbins
Baker's Lane
Knowle
Warwickshire B93 8PR
01564 730199

Heal Farm Quality Meats
Kingsnympton
Umberleigh
Devon EX37 9TB
01769 574341

C. Lidgate
110 Holland Park Avenue
London W11 4UA
0171 727 8243

Loch Shin Game of Scotland
3 Terryside
Shinness
Lairg
Sutherland IV27 4DL
01549 2300

Luddesdown Organic Farms Ltd
Court Lodge
Luddesdown
Cobham
Kent DA13 0XE
01474 813376

Macbeth's
11 Tolbooth Street
Forres Moray
Scotland IV36 0PH

Makentie Ltd
Back Lane
Newburgh
Lancashire WN8 7TH
01257 462450

Makro Multi-Trade Centre
Emerson House
Albert Street
Eccles
Manchester M30 0LJ
0161 707 1585

McCartney's Family Butchers
Main Street
Moira
Co Down
Northern Ireland

Godfrey Meynell
Meynell Langley
Kirk Langley
Derby DE6 4NT
01332 824207

Mrs Lam's Delicious Food Company
Unit 1F to 1K
Aintree Racecourse
Business Park
Aintree, Liverpool
Merseyside L9 5AY
0151 523 0777

North Devon Meat Ltd
School Lane
Torrington
Devon EX38 7EX
01805 23371

H & S Openshaw
Fisherman's Wharf
Nile Street
Bolton
Lancashire BL3 6BW
01204 534585

The Organic Food Club
7 Dudley Villas
Cleeve Road
Marlcliff
Bidford-on-Avon
Warks B50 4NR
01789 772870

Orkney Meat Ltd
Grainshore Road
Hatston
Kirkwall
Orkney KW15 1FL
01856 874326

A.S. Portwine & Son
Graham Portwine
24 Earlham Street
London WC2H 9LN
0171 836 2353

Real Meat Co. Ltd
East Hill Farm
Heylesbury
Warminster
Wiltshire BA12 0HR
01985 40436

Donald Russell
6 Jardine House
The Harrovian Business
Village
Bessborough Road
Harrow HA1 3EX
0181 422 3400

Scotch Premier Meat
63 Woodend Place
Aberdeen
Scotland AB15 6AP
01224 311874

G.G Sparkes
Guy & Gemma Sparkes
(Organic Butchers)
24 Old Dover Road
Blackheath
London SE3 7BT
0181 355 8597

St. Marcus Fine Foods & Butchers
1 Rockingham Close
London SW15 5RW

Arnold Sudaby & Co
P.O. Box 5, Hartland
Bideford
Devon EX39 6YT

Vin Sullivan Foods Ltd
2 Gilchrist
Thomas Esate
Blaenavon
Gwent NP4 9RL
012495 792792

Wensleydale Wild Boar Breeders
Heron Cottage
Manor Farm
Thornton Steward
Ripon
North Yorkshire HG4 4BB
01677 60239

OTHER USEFUL INFORMATION

The British Meat Information Service
Gill Spivey
59 Russell Square
London WC1 4HJ
0171 631 3434

British Organic Farmers
86 Coston Street
Bristol BS1 5BB
01272 299666

British Standards Institution
2 Park Street
London W1A 2BS
0171 629 9000

Chartered Institute of Environmental Health
Chadwick Court
15 Hatfield Road
London SE1 8DJ
0171 827 5868

The Chefs & Cooks Circles
PO Box 239
London N14 7NT
0181 368 3237

Department of Health
Richmond House
79 Whitehall
London SW1A 2NS
0171 210 3000

Euro-Torques (U.K. Chapter)
Administrative Office
Winteringham Fields
Winteringham
North Lincolnshire DN15 9PF

Farmers' Weekly
Quadrant House
Sutton, Surrey SM2 5AS
0181 652 4911

Fiswal Catering Equipment
Mark Walls
Empress Works
Penny Lane, Haydock
St Helens
Merseyside WA11 0QU
01942 713377

Food Marketing & Manufacturing Magazine
Yandell Publishing Ltd
8 Vermont Place
Tongwell
Milton Keynes MK15 8JA
01908 613323

Louise Ayling
Game Marketing Executive
0171 642 9343

Guild of Q Butchers
Ross Muir Public Relations
7 Dunfermiline Road
Limekilns
Fife KY11 3JU
01383 872988

The Humane Slaughter Association
34 Blanche Lane
South Mimms
Potters Bar
Herts EN6 3PA
01707 659040

International Food Development Chef & Catering Advisor
0589 111256

Life Magazines
Oyston Mill
Strand Road
Preston, Lancashire PR1 8UR
01722 722022

The Meat & Livestock Commission
PO Box 44
Winterhill House
Snowdon Drive
Milton Keynes
Bucks MK6 1AX
01908 609826

Meat Training Council
PO Box 141
Winterhill House
Snowdon Drive
Milton Keynes
Bucks MK6 1YY
01908 231062

National Association of Catering Butchers
217 Central Markets
Smithfield
London EC1A 9LH
0171 489 0005

National Federation of Meat & Food Traders
1 Belgrove Road
Tunbridge Wells
Kent TN1 1YW
01892 541412

The National Game Dealers Association
1 Belgrove Road
Tunbridge Wells
Kent TN1 1YW
01892 541412

Neff UK Ltd
Grand Union House
Old Wolverton Road, Old Wolverton
Milton Keynes
Buckinghamshire MK12 5PT

Organic Food Federation
The Tithe House
Peaseland Green
Elsing
East Dereham
Norfolk NR20 3DY
01362 637314

Red Velvet Beetroot
Kershaws Farm
Smithy Lane
Scarisbrick
Lancashire L40 8HN
01704 840392

Rediveg
Oliver Kay
Fisherman's Wharf
Nile Street
Bolton
Lancashire BL3 6BW
01204 385463

Ricon Ingredients & Technical Systems For the Food Industry
Paul Smyth
Unit 4, Morris Green
Business Park
Fearnhead Street, St Helens Road
Bolton
Lancashire BL3 3PE

The Scottish Quality Beef & Lamb Association
Vic Prow, UK Promotions Manager
Rural Centre, West Mains, Ingliston
Newbridge, Midlothian EH28 8NZ
0131 472 4040

Shooting and Conversation
Marford Mill
Rossett
Wrexham, Clwyd LL12 0HL
01244 573000

Shooting Times
Kings' Reach Tower
Stamford Street
London SE1 9LS
0171 261 6180

The Yandell Food & Meat Media Group
8 Vermont Place
Tongwell
Milton Keynes MK15 8JA
01908 613323

INDEX

bacon:
Creamy Grouse Pie with Bacon and Shallots 121
David Niven's *Cailles Rôties sur Canapés* 38
Partridge Suprêmes Princess Royal 32
Pigeons in Pimlico 45
Roast Grouse with Bacon and Sauce Chasseur Garnished
   with Dripping Triangles 47
Sussex Houghed Pheasant and Grouse Breasts with Smoked
   Bacon 27
Terrine of Hare and Ham with a Rich Cranberry and Shallot
   Marmalade 134
Wild Trout Fillets with Bacon and Almond Sauce 107
Wild Trout with Almonds, Apples and Smoked Bacon 106
birds:
drawing 10
hanging 9
jointing 10
plucking 10
trussing 10–11
blackcock:
Pheasant and Blackcock Casserole with Wild Mushrooms
   and Shallots 28
Roast Blackcock with Raspberry Sauce 50
boar *see* wild boar
Bordelaise Sauce 144
bread:
Fried Breadcrumbs 151
Traditional Bread Sauce 147
Butter, Clarified 151

Cailles aux Raisins 39
Cailles Rôties sur Canapés 38
capercailzie: Roast Capercailzie with Orange and Cranberry
   Stuffing 49
Cheese Scone Pastry 154
Clarified Butter 151
Court-bouillon 142
Cranberry Sauce 145
curries:
Creamy Hare and Wild Mushroom Curry 77
Prelice sa Pirincem (Quail in a Coconut Curry Sauce) 42
Rabbit Curry 70
Wild Boar Curry with Lime and Rosemary 96

Demi-glace Sauce 143
duck 12
Braised Drunken Duck 18
Breast of Gressingham Duckling Baked in Lemon Marmalade
   14
Chinese Egg Noodles with Duck 17
Crusty Baked Long Island Duck 19
Duck and Pea Soup 113
Julian Groom's Breast of Gressingham Duckling with
   Amaretto Sauce 15
Peking Duckling 16

Roast Duckling 13
Smooth Duck and Pigeon Pâté 130
Wild Duckling with Oranges and Rose-Petal Vinegar 20
duck livers:
Duck Livers with Raspberry and Amaretto Sauce on a Bed of
   Bubble and Squeak Cakes 23
Julian Groom's Potted Game 132
Smooth Duck and Pigeon Pâté 130
Terrine of Woodcock 133

Espagnole Sauce 143

fish:
boning 99
cleaning 99
filleting 99
Fish Court-bouillon 142
food safety 7

game:
Cream of Game Soup 110
European Game Marinade 140
Game Consommé 110
Game Soup with Sherry 112
Game Stock 141
Game Stuffing 149
Julian Groom's Potted Game 132
Olde English Game Terrine 131
Onion and Game Tart 129
seasons 7
Game Chips 149
giblets:
Giblet Gravy 148
Giblet Stock 142
Scotland the Brave Giblet Soup 111
goose 56
Maryland Style Goose Breast 58
Roast Goose with Mint, Onion and Apple Stuffing 56–7
Roast Goose with Orange Brandy Sauce 57
Gravy, Giblet 148
grouse 47
Creamy Grouse Pie with Bacon and Shallots 121
Grouse in Port Pie 122
Honey Roast Grouse with Chestnuts and Game Chips 48
Roast Grouse with Bacon and Sauce Chasseur Garnished
   with Dripping Triangles 47
Sussex Houghed Pheasant and Grouse Breasts with Smoked
   Bacon 27
Traditional Christmas Jugged Turkey 63
guinea fowl 51
Guinea Fowl and Pork with Tarragon and Cider Sauce 54
Guinea Fowl and Vermicelli Soup 112–13
Roast Guinea Fowl 51
Roast Guinea Fowl and Cranberry Pie 123
Stir-fried Guinea Fowl 55

Suprême of Guinea Fowl Nell Gwynn 53
A Tenor's Fried Guinea Fowl 52

ham:
Partridge Suprêmes Princess Royal 32
Rabbit and Ham Pie 124
Terrine of Hare and Ham with a Rich Cranberry and Shallot
Marmalade 134
hare 74
Creamy Hare and Wild Mushroom Curry 77
Devonshire Hare Pie 126
Hare Casserole 74
Hare in a Mushroom and Burgundy Sauce 76
Jugged Hare with Potato Herb Dumplings 75
skinning 65
Terrine of Hare and Ham with a Rich Cranberry and Shallot
Marmalade 134
Terrine of Wild Rabbit 133
Hot Water Pastry 152
hunting 79

kebabs:
English Eldon Blue Pork Kebabs with English Mustard 92
Spanish Wild Boar Kebabs 92
Kipper Salmon (Smoked Salmon) 100–1

lobster: Suprêmes of Partridge Filled with Lobster 33

Madeira Sauce 145
marinades:
European Game Marinade 140
Tom's Marinade for Game 139
White Wine, Honey and Garlic Marinade 140

ovens: Circotherm temperature conversion chart 155

partridge 30
Braised Breast of Partridge Filled with Wild Boar Sausage
and Mushrooms 34
Grilled Partridge 30
Partridge Suprêmes Princess Royal 32
Rigatoni and Pesto Baked Partridge 35
Roast Partridge 30
Roast Partridge in Chive and Brandy Cream 31
Suprêmes of Partridge Filled with Lobster 33
pastry 152
Cheese Scone Pastry 154
Hot Water Pastry 152
Puff Pastry 153
Rosa Lewis's Suet Pastry 153
Shortcrust Pastry 152
pâtés 130
Hart of England Smooth Venison Pâté 135
Smoked Wild Trout and Beetroot Pâté 137
Smooth Duck and Pigeon Pâté 130
pheasant 24
Festive Mustard Baked Pheasant 26
Pheasant with Baby Onions and Green Peas 26–7
Pheasant and Blackcock Casserole with Wild Mushrooms
and Shallots 28
Pheasant and Mushroom Pie 119
Pheasant and Wild Mushroom Pie with Two Pastries 118
Roast Pheasant Breasts in Coriander Cream 25

Roast Pheasant with Calvados and Apples 24
Scotland the Brave Giblet Soup 111
Sussex Houghed Pheasant and Grouse Breasts with Smoked
Bacon 27
Wholemeal Spaghetti with Suprême of Pheasant 29
pies and tarts 117
Cold Rabbit Pie with Apple, Almonds and Port 125
Creamy Grouse Pie with Bacon and Shallots 121
Devonshire Hare Pie 126
Grouse in Port Pie 122
Lancashire Pigeon Pie 120
My Favourite Venison and Chestnut Pie 128
My Hunting Herb Pie 127
Onion and Game Tart 129
Pheasant and Mushroom Pie 119
Pheasant and Wild Mushroom Pie with Two Pastries 118
Rabbit and Ham Pie 124
Roast Guinea Fowl and Cranberry Pie 123
pigeon 43
Grilled Breast of Pigeon with a Peach Salad and Hazelnut
Dressing 44
Lancashire Pigeon Pie 120
Pigeon with Figs 43
Pigeons in Pimlico 45
Pigeons in Red Wine 46
Smooth Duck and Pigeon Pâté 130
pork:
English Eldon Blue Pork Kebabs with English Mustard 92
Guinea Fowl and Pork with Tarragon and Cider Sauce 54
Hart of England Smooth Venison Pâté 135
My Hunting Herb Pie 127
Olde English Game Terrine 131
Rillettes of Eldon Blue Pork 136
Roast Loin of Eldon Blue Pork with Bordelaise Sauce 93
Spit-roast Loin of Eldon Blue Pork 91
Terrine of Hare and Ham with a Rich Cranberry and Shallot
Marmalade 134
Terrine of Wild Rabbit 133
Thai Stir-Fried Eldon Blue Pork with Pasta and Vegetables 95
Potato Cakes 150
Potted Game, Julian Groom's 132
prawns: Freshly Poached Wild Salmon in Aspic with Freshwater
Prawn and Asparagus Salad 102
Prelice sa Pirincem (Quail in a Coconut Curry Sauce) 42
Puff Pastry 153

quail 36
Cailles aux Raisins 39
David Niven's Cailles Rôties sur Canapés 38
Joan Whittle's Quail with Mushrooms 36
Prelice sa Pirincem (Quail in a Coconut Curry Sauce) 42
Quail Peking Style 40
Quail and Rabbit Casserole 41
Rosa's Honey Roast Quail with Mint and Garlic 37
Rosa's Quail Pudding 40–1
quail eggs 38

rabbit 66
Braised Rabbit with Black Pudding and Cider Sauce 68
Casserole of Venison and Rabbit County Wicklow Style 88
Cold Rabbit Pie with Apple, Almonds and Port 125
Grouse in Port Pie 122
Quail and Rabbit Casserole 41

Rabbit Cacciatore with Basil and Sun-Blush Tomatoes 69
Rabbit Cooked in Port with a Rum and Raisin Sauce 66–7
Rabbit Curry 70
Rabbit with Fusilli 73
Rabbit and Ham Pie 124
Rabbit Jambalaya 71
Rabbit (or Hare) Casserole 74
Rabbit with Rosemary Cider Sauce 67
Rigatoni with Rabbit and Cream Sauce 72
Roasted Rabbit 66
skinning 65
Terrine of Wild Rabbit 133
Tom's Rabbit Soup 114
Red Cabbage 147
Relish, Yorkshire 146
rillettes 130
Rillettes of Eldon Blue Pork 136
Rowan Jelly 146

salmon 100
Freshly Poached Wild Salmon in Aspic with Freshwater
Prawn and Asparagus Salad 102
Individual Terrines of Wild Scottish Salmon 137
Kipper Salmon (Smoked Salmon) 100–1
Poached Salmon with Orange and Basil Sauce 103
Wild Salmon Fillets Filled with Leek and Parsley 104
Wild Salmon Soup 115
Wild Salmon Steaks in Foil 101
Wild Salmon and Tuna Fishcakes 105
sauces:
Bordelaise Sauce 144
Demi-glace Sauce 143
Espagnole Sauce 143
Giblet Gravy 148
Home-made Cranberry Sauce 145
Madeira Sauce 145
Sauce Chasseur 144
Sauce Poivrade 145
Traditional Bread Sauce 147
sausages/sausagemeat:
Braised Breast of Partridge Filled with Wild Boar Sausage
and Mushrooms 34
Game Stuffing 149
Venison Burgers 89
Wild Boar Sausage Pot with Paprika 97
Shortcrust Pastry 152
soups 109
Cream of Game Soup 110
Duck and Pea Soup 113
Game Consommé 110
Game Soup with Sherry 112
Guinea Fowl and Vermicelli Soup 112–13
Scotland the Brave Giblet Soup 111
Tom's Rabbit Soup 114
Venison Broth 114
Wild Salmon Soup 115
stocks 141
Game Stock 141
Giblet Stock 142
Stuffing, Game 149
Suet Pastry 153

tarts *see* pies and tarts

teal:
Roast Teal 21
Teal Breasts in Creamed Brandy with Honey and Lemon 22
terrines 117, 130
Individual Terrines of Wild Scottish Salmon 137
Olde English Game Terrine 131
Terrine of Hare and Ham with a Rich Cranberry and Shallot
Marmalade 134
Terrine of Wild Rabbit 132
Terrine of Woodcock 133
trout 106
Smoked Wild Trout and Beetroot Pâté 137
Wild Trout Fillets with Bacon and Almond Sauce 107
Wild Trout with Almonds, Apples and Smoked Bacon 106
Truffle Oil 151
tuna: Wild Salmon and Tuna Fishcakes 106
turkey:
Breast of Wild Turkey with Sun-Blush Tomatoes 61
Breast of Wild Turkey with a White Wine and Black Cherry
Sauce 60
Sticky Breast of Turkey 63
Traditional Christmas Jugged Turkey 62
Turkey Bourguignon 62–3
Wild Turkey with Caramelized Onion and Apple 59

venison 80
Baked Venison Cutlets with Oyster Mushrooms 87
Casserole of Venison and Rabbit County Wicklow Style 88
Game Soup with Sherry 113
Game Stock 141
Hart of England Smooth Venison Pâté 135
My Favourite Venison and Chestnut Pie 128
Olde English Game Terrine 131
Oven-Baked Venison Steaks with Mustard 86
Roast Loin of Venison 82
Sophia's Choice 84
Traditional Roast Venison 81
Traditional Scottish Venison Hotpot 89
Venison Bolognese 90
Venison Broth 114
Venison Burgers 89
Venison Spare Ribs with Garlic Sauce 83
Venison Steaks with Garlic and Five-Spice 85
venison livers: Hart of England Smooth Venison Pâté 135

wild boar 91
Carbonnade of Wild Boar with Guinness 94
English Eldon Blue Pork Kebabs with English Mustard 92
My Hunting Herb Pie 127
Olde English Game Terrine 131
Rillettes of Eldon Blue Pork 136
Roast Loin of Eldon Blue Pork with Bordelaise Sauce 93
Spanish Wild Boar Kebabs 92
Spit-roast Loin of Eldon Blue Pork 91
Thai Stir-Fried Eldon Blue Pork with Pasta and Vegetables 95
Wild Boar Curry with Lime and Rosemary 96
Wild Boar Risotto 94
Wild Boar Sausage Pot with Paprika 97
Woodcock, Terrine of 132–3

Yorkshire Relish 146